BECOMING A BESTSELLER

The Proven Path to Your Bestseller in 60 Days

CHARLES SCHWARTZ

WITH

CHRISTINE ZAFRA

Published by AuthorsUnite.com

TABLE OF CONTENTS

INTRODUCTION

This is not a manuscript about writing books. A book like that is a waste of time. This is a book about generating leverage, influence, and massive income. We live in a world of hidden access, unknown paths, and secret treasures. Within are the closely guarded keys that every successful person has access to. Ones you are about to discover.

What follows is the framework that will change the way you approach your book, business, and perhaps the way you live your life.

For the past decade, I have helped countless entrepreneurs retire and build enough passive income that their children no longer need to worry about income. This is just one of the strategies I have leveraged to help them accomplish the dreams they once though out of reach.

To get the most out of this book, I encourage you to do only three things:

1. Read the book in its entirety and embrace the concepts within
2. Take massive action with the tools that we will provide to you for FREE
3. Let go of perfection as it is the enemy of progress.

The world has changed. We invite people into our lives which once was considered taboo and forbidden. Your potential customers are begging you to be the heroic guide that will rescue them. They need to hear your voice, your story, and have access to your services. Only those who are willing to be in service to others above themselves will be rewarded.

Before we start, make sure you head over to:

- The **Becoming a Bestseller** website at **www.becomingabestseller.com** and get access to your *Path to Publish* resource guide
- The **Becoming a Bestseller Facebook** page and join us, along with fellow aspiring bestselling authors, and find an accountability partner, resources, support, and more.

WHY MOST PEOPLE WILL NEVER FINISH THEIR BOOK

Most people waste an enormous amount of time and money writing and marketing their book. We all know how difficult, soul crushing, and costly it is to try and get our dream from our heads to the market. Worse yet, the ones that do have their hard work disappear into the abyss of mediocrity if they are ever read at all.

What if the problem was not how well your book was written? What if the problem was the way we thought about the entire book and its launch?

The problem is simple. For so many of us, we approach life in the opposite order. Many of us shoot an arrow and then, long after the arrow has left our hands, we ask ourselves where we would like it to go. It is like getting on an airplane and turning to the passenger next to you and saying "Gosh, I hope this goes somewhere amazing!" How many of us start with the end in mind? How many of us understand the true power of the book we are creating? The marketing, the sales funnels, and the possibilities for upsell?

The fact is, pretty covers alone don't sell books. Words burned into sentences are not enough. If you have not clarified your intent before you even show up, your clients won't even know you exist. We have all read books that sit on the New York Times Bestseller list that leave us dumbfounded on how they got there in the first place.

Yet year after year, we pay small fortunes to design firms, and copy editors, and plead with publishing companies. For so many of us, we are lost in the dream of: If my books become a bestseller, I will have *made it*. So few of us truly know the real power of being a bestseller, and even less, know how to wield its true strength.

Here at **B**ecoming **A B**est**S**eller (BABS), we have clients that hit the lists and develop a six-figure income time and time again. Remember, no one will listen to you if they cannot find you, your message is not clear, and you don't give them a clear path to take. The BABS model is as effective for multi-millionaires as it is for the first-time authors within us all.

The reality is, we are not just in a race to finish our books, or ensure we don't have an inferior message, but that we have a plan that will help us achieve our goals.

So what is the purpose of your book? Who is your market? Do they know what to do once they buy your book? Can anyone look at your model at any point and clearly determine your goals in a way that is compelling and invigorating? Did you struggle to answer those questions? How many opportunities are we losing because we don't have these answers?

By the end of our journey together, you will never struggle with them again.

It is time to take inventory and clarify where we are going. Throughout this book we will reference the BABS Model which we call the *Path to Publish*, its worksheets, and bonus materials. Make sure you don't miss out on these FREE recourses that change everything at www.becomingabestseller.com.

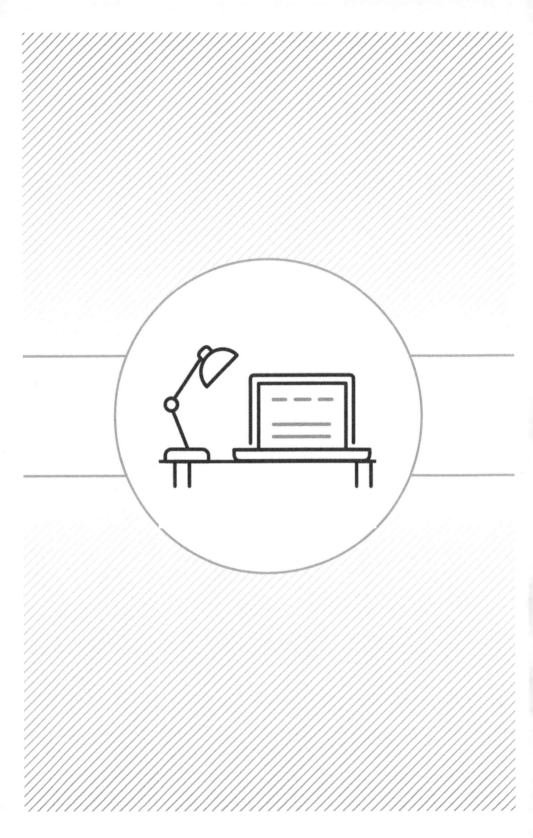

PRODUCE

1

WHY

SO MANY

AUTHORS

FAIL

ooks are the new business cards. In Japan, there is a ritual of exchanging meishi, Japanese for 'business card'. This is a practice revered in Japan, far beyond what it is in the West. The exchanging of business cards, like other ceremonies in Japan, is based on order, status, and rank. This means there is a hierarchical order, which must be followed, that governs business card exchange. Knowing the intimate details of this secret procedural order can define your success or failure. Business cards are leverage in the east, while in the west, we now have books. In the past it was having a college degree. Then it was having a master's degree, which then was fortified by what prestigious Ivy League school you attended. What if there was a way to circumvent the years of study and the six-figure student loan debt? There is.

Enter Abraham Maslow and his hierarchy of needs. Our primitive brain is constantly looking for a way to ensure we are safe, fed, and part of a group. That we are somehow enough, protected, and if we are lucky, loved. In the 1960s, that meant a good job and dependable income. Now in the age of social media and over-sharing, that has now expanded to include social proof. How, you ask? Just take in these two shocking facts about American consumers (also known as your target audience):

- Over 70% of Americans say they look at product reviews before making a purchase.[1]
- Nearly 63% of consumers indicate they are more likely to purchase from a site if it has product ratings and reviews.[2]

Think of it another way:

Two people are applying for a job:

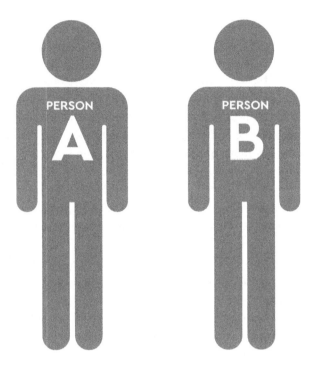

Person A went to a good school and has similar experience as Person B.

Person B went to a lesser school but wrote a book on the topic this job covers and it became a Bestseller on Amazon, USA Today, and *The New York Times*.

Who gets the job?

What if it was a paid speaking opportunity? The person selling a course?

How powerful is social proof? Take, for example, a study done by the Wall Street Journal[3]:

A group of researchers examined the effectiveness on persuading customers to use less energy in the summer. In order to accomplish this, they wanted them to use their fans instead of air conditioning. The test was simple and leveraged 4 types of signs:

1 The first sign informed the customers that they could save $54/month on their utility bill by using the fans.

2 The second sign informed the customers that by using fans, they could reduce the amount of greenhouse gas by 262 pounds each and every month.

3 The third sign told the customers that using the fans was the responsible thing to do.

4 The fourth and final sign stated that 77% of their neighbors were already using fans to save energy.

So which sign was the most effective? That's right, you guessed it: The Fourth Sign. Why? Because positive social proof is more persuasive than saving money, protecting the environment, or making responsible choices. Starting to understand why becoming a bestseller changes everything?

Remember if you are not leveraging your book in a way that somehow makes your audience feed themselves, find love, or belong to a tribe, you are ineffective and most likely to fail.

MISTAKE NUMBER ONE — YOUR BOOK MUST HAVE A PURPOSE LARGER THAN YOU

There are three reasons to write a book, but they must meet a single goal for your audience. Your book must somehow help them thrive, survive, or escape. Without this it will fall flat.

PURPOSE #1 — PASSION PROJECT

You have a story within you. Something that only you can tell. Maybe it is your personal story of surviving through tragedy, the back story of your family, or one that has blossomed in your own mind for decades. When writing your story, to simply write your story is enough. Remember, you never have to do anything in this lifetime to be enough or be deserving of love. However, if you wish to become a bestseller, you must meet your audience's needs. Still, just like becoming a bestseller, there is a Path to Publish to that success as well. In Christopher Booker's book, The Seven Basic Plots, he describes in detail nine basic plots for all great story-telling. He also, in his title, understood the rules of 3,5,7. The human mind adores things that are kept in 3,5,7. Anything beyond that and we get confused. With that in mind, he names his book with the number seven, but really had nine. In time, knowing how the human mind is hard-coded to work will radically change your success. Anyway, back to Chris and his seven, oops, nine plots that are proven for success:

1. **Overcoming the Monster:** In this story, our hero must track down and battle the monster that is threatening something he cares for. The hero then destroys the monster and escapes with the righteous rewards.

2. **Rags to Riches:** This version starts with a commoner who discovers his or her hidden potential for greatness and manages to rise to a potential beyond their dreams.

3. **The Quest:** Our hero sets forth on a pursuit to obtain an illustrious prize, far, far away.

4. **Voyage and Return:** Wanderlust for a new, enchanting, and strange world lures our hero away from home, only for him to face struggles that force him to come back home and realize the beauty that was taken for granted.

5. **Comedy:** Normally based around a community divided by frustration, selfishness, confusion, lack of self-discovery, and lies, only to be bonded together by love and harmony.

6. **Tragedy:** Where our hero faces the loss of affluence because of a terminal error.

7. **Rebirth:** Where our hero is freed from an opposing force that traps him in a living hell until he/she is saved by a different character's action.

8. **Rebellion Against 'The One':** In this version, our hero fights back against an omnipotent villain, bent on controlling the world until forced into defeat.

9. **Mystery:** Where our lead discovers the truth to a normally tragic event.

PURPOSE #2 – LEVERAGING OR BRANDING

Welcome to cognitive bias, specifically the halo effect. Science teaches us that we are far more likely to judge a person's opinion on the overall perception of him or her. The most common place we do this is in judging someone based on their attractiveness. Simply put, if we see a photograph of a person who looks attractive, well-groomed, and dressed well, our minds immediately assume that person is a good person and their opinion has more merit. It does not stop there; if the overall social concept of the individual's preferences is viewed as high, we will value their products or services higher. When people ask me what I do, I normally say "I coach entrepreneurs on how to retire." When I am on stage I normally start every speech with: "Hello, I am Charles Schwartz and grew up 'P', as I could not afford the last three letters of 'poor'. However, I retired at 36, become a millionaire at 37, and was invited to lecture at Yale at 38." This is using the halo effect, because I am leveraging the success and opportunities not for my ego, but for my audience. For most, when they hear this, they immediately think: "What! How did he go from poor to a millionaire? I am not that poor, heck, I have advantages over this guy. I need to find out so I can be free as well. I am going to ask him." Remember it is not about what you sell, it is what you solve for your audience.

Writing a book and becoming a bestseller also define you as a subject expert in your book's chosen field. If you want to get a job working for Google, would it help to have a bestseller on search engine algorithms? If you were the bestseller in your local market, would that not be something you could leverage into television interviews? Podcasts? YouTube? Of course it will, and that generates followers. The more followers you have, the larger your audience that you can leverage towards your ultimate goal.

There are 7 rules that you must adhere to before you decide to leverage your personal brand[4]:

1. DEFINE YOUR NICHE:

This means a clear and focused message that clearly targets a well-defined audience. This must be based on three things:
i. What do they want?
ii. What is blocking or preventing them from getting it?
iii. What dream life will they obtain once they achieve their goal?

2. AUTHENTICITY:

We have all seen the ads where someone disingenuous has rented a house and/or cars, saying how amazing or wealthy he is, just because he read a book or took a course. Not only is this vile, but it is transparent. Coming across as relatable and trustworthy will skyrocket your brand. Simply put, be you. Share who you are and what you love, and in time your audience will flock to you.

3. BE A TOUR GUIDE:

People want to be taken on a magical journey that solves their problems, or at the very least, shows them how someone else has. Remember if you are not telling your audience a story or helping them buy into an identity, you have already lost before you have begun. Your audience does not want to hear how amazing, rich, or successful you are. They want to know how they can accomplish what you have, or escape into your world, if even for a few pages. How many of our audience are buying someone else's books even though we know deep down it is garbage? They are, because of two reasons; better marketing and/or better story telling.

4. DEPENDABILITY:

Your brand must be consistent with what it is saying, when it is saying it and how it is saying it. This includes online and offline. For example, if you are showing yourself next to a private jet and fancy cars, yet the next post is you flying coach, you have just lost your audience's trust. If you are preaching about how disgusting wearing fur is, only to be seen wearing a fur coat the next day, poof...credibility is gone. Choose a message, stay on point. If you choose colors, a time of day you post, and how your content comes across, your audience will reward you.

5. EMBRACE FAILURE:

Surprise! You are going to fail. Over and over and over and over again.

It is inevitable and predictable. However, although most people run from this, effective branders embrace it with loving arms. Remember the plot type of rebirth? We all love a good story of someone making it to the top, failing and then having the ability to once again rise to the top. Nobody can resist a good story. So much so that neuroscientists have discovered that we spend over 30% of our time daydreaming. FAIL FASTER! You, your book, and your brand will reap the benefits.

6. BE IMPACTFUL:

Ever heard of Dwayne Johnson, also known as "The Rock"? Sure, he is a villain from time to time on the World Wrestling Entertainment (WWE) stage, but in real life he is renowned as being a positive man. His work, his charity, and his time are routinely given to causes and his fans. Ensure you are leveraging your brand as one that consistently is in service of your audience and the causes they believe in. You and your brand reputation will determine what leverage points you can use in the future and how successful your book ultimately becomes.

7. FOLLOW THE LEADER:

We have all played this game as a child. One of the other kids on the playground does an action and we mirror it. Somehow in life, we have forgotten this concept, that success leaves clues. Look for someone who's success inspires you. Then do everything you can to learn from them. What did they do? How did they write their book? What inspires you about them? Once you have discovered their formula, be authentic and build your own with that inspiration. Never steal and always pay homage to the source.

PURPOSE #3 — MONEY

To help grow your way to becoming a bestseller, we are going to guide you through a simplified process. However, we need to get really honest about why you are writing this book in the first place. If your goal is income, then own it. Here is a reality check; just over 50% of all authors make less than $15,000 per year and roughly 17% make nothing.[5] Why does this happen? Because authors are not normally business-focused. Their focus is selling thousands of books for $25, with a minimal profit after printing and shipping costs, instead of understanding their book is marketing material to sell their course, coaching, or opportunity for thousands. There is a simple way to think about it:

You need **5,000** people to buy a **$200** product.

You need **2,000** people to buy a **$500** product.

You need **1,000** people to buy a **$1,000** product.

You need **500** people to buy a **$2,000** product.

You need **300** people to buy a **$3,333** product.

You need **200** people to buy a **$5,000** product.

You need **100** people to buy a **$10,000** product.

You need **50** people to buy a **$20,000** product.

You need **25** people to buy a **$40,000** product.

You need **5** people to buy a **$200,000** product.

Can you build a series, sell coaching, or get booked as a professional speaker? Far too many authors fail to understand the rules have changed and having their income based purely on book sales alone is a rare feat. However, there are 5 key ways to have your bestseller earn you income:

1. Passive income in the form of a series. (i.e. multiple books)
2. Have your book establish you as a content expert increasing your rate as a speaker
3. As a marketing sales funnel
4. A precursor to your courses, coaching, or professional seminars
5. Increase your social following base to raise your endorsement offers and fees.

Our team has successfully created over 700 bestselling authors and a good deal of them are making solid six figures a year. The ones who have leveled up started with a choice. A choice to break free from mediocrity and complacency. To fully embrace the BABS model, find a mentor, and build a dedicated plan.

NEXT STEPS

Guarantee your successful launch and revenue stream
- Go to becomingabestseller.com and either create a free account or log in to your existing Path to Publish.
- Sit down and brainstorm the plot of your book. Who is the book for? What do they want and what is preventing them from getting it?
- How does your book help them thrive towards their dreams and goals?
- Discover your true purpose for writing your book and what systems you would like to have once it is written.

Once you begin your journey on the Path to Publish, you'll be on your way to becoming a bestseller. One that serves their audience from a place of authenticity and clarity. Beginning to define what they really need and want. Of course it is natural to want to fill out the entire Path to Publish, however take your time. Read the next chapter and stay in line with our progress so far.

MISTAKE NUMBER TWO — FEAR, FAILURE AND LIMITING BELIEFS: ALL TOOLS WE NEED TO SUCCEED

"Fear is not real. The only place that fear can exist is in our thoughts of the future. It is a product of our imagination, causing us to fear things that do not at present and may not ever exist. That is near insanity. Do not misunderstand me; danger is very real but fear is a choice."[6]

— Will Smith

Fear

Wikipedia defines fear as:

Fear is a feeling induced by perceived danger or threat that occurs in certain types of organisms, which causes a change in metabolic and organ functions and ultimately a change in behavior, such as fleeing, hiding, or freezing from perceived traumatic events. Fear in human beings may occur in response to a certain stimulus occurring in the present, or in anticipation or expectation of a future threat perceived as a risk to body or life. The fear response arises from the per-

ception of danger leading to confrontation with or escape from/avoiding the threat (also known as the fight-or-flight response), which in extreme cases of fear (horror and terror) can be a freeze response or paralysis.[7]

Fear is also broken down by two creative acronyms:
1. F.E.A.R. = Forget Everything And Run
2. F.E.A.R. = Face Everything And Rise

In my first book, *Who Changes Everything*, we spend a great deal of time breaking down the power of fear as a fuel source. One that tells us where we are lacking and what we are unprepared for. A fuel source that can burn true enough to get us started, but will never by itself get us to our goals. Facing our fears, with their corresponding limiting beliefs, and listening to them is critical in becoming a bestseller.

FIRST LIMITING BELIEF: TIME

The most common source of doubt for most aspiring authors is time. We have all said, "I just don't have enough time to finish the book." We all have enough time and intuitively we all know we can solve this problem. So, what are we really saying?

I don't really want to make the time to write this book.

The average person can write 1,000 words a day, or 30,000k a month. If a dedicated author spent 30 minutes in the morning and 30 minutes in the evening, they would have a solid book in under sixty days. So what are you really saying? Do you really want to write this book? There is a huge difference between "want" and "willing". For example, I want to climb Mount Everest, however I am not willing to sit on a plane for 36+ hours just to fly there. That is before even reaching the mountain to begin climbing! What are you willing to do? What sacrifices are you willing to make to achieve your dream?

WORTHINESS

As we discussed before, life is simple and comes down to: Am I enough? And if so, am I worthy of being loved? These are just two of the many questions we ask ourselves over and over, throughout every hour of everyday. Here is a bonus secret: You are. You always have been. There is nothing you need to do to be worthy or loved. Notice the period at the end of that sentence? It is that simple. You don't need to write a book, become president, or reach some goal to be deserving of love. What you might want to do is get extremely honest with yourself. Are you an expert, that knows every single thing on the topic you are writing on? Probably not. For most of us, we are not source, we are synthesis. It is our voice and our interpretation of the material. No one can be you. More so it is not about them or their opinion. Put it out there, have it fail, do a revision, have it fail, then repeat. Most people think writing a book has a beginning and a solid end. However, one of the few things that people talk about are the revisions and the updated versions. Remember perfection is the enemy of execution.

WON'T LIKE YOUR WORK

Most authors have a fear that their book will suck or will get bad reviews. Here is another secret: it will. Some will think your book is horrible and possibly the worst thing a certain person has ever read. At least for a few people it will and they might make a lot of noise. Heck, there are people who don't like the Harry Potter books and think J. K. Rowling is a sham! There will be people out there that give you bad reviews and hate your work. It is going to happen. Writing a book is not a popularity contest. Steve Jobs once said, "If you want to make everyone happy, don't be a leader, sell ice cream". This is your book, your dream, and your future. What others think of you does not define you. Just don't be surprised when the negative reviews come in. Simple advice is not to read them.

I CAN'T AFFORD TO

This is one we hear all the time. We have made people bestsellers with a budget of less than $500. However, lets change the comment and question. What is your real goal? Can you become a New York Times Self-Published Bestseller for $500? Probably not. What about the Wall Street Journal? Or USA Today? Again, probably not. Sadly, much like so many other things in life, you have to pay to play. There are certain milestones, connections, and goals that must be met. This is the exact reason we put together this book and provided you the Path to Publish on Becoming a Bestseller. However, if you play the long game, there are tools and strategies that will allow the book to pay for itself. We will review the strategic partnerships, cost-cutting solutions, and relationships that will pay for your book to be written. For now, always remember when building relationships, to ask yourself:

How are you helping them succeed
and get what they want?

We have broken the process down where we have a guaranteed bestseller program. We will share access to our program that will allow you to become a bestselling co-author for less than $300.

MISTAKE NUMBER THREE — GOING IN ALONE WITHOUT ACCOUNTABILITY

*"If you want to go fast, go alone.
If you want to go far, go together."*

— Unknown

Accountability is making a choice, measuring them against your core values and beliefs, and then holding yourself to your commitment. The issue is that it takes will-power and will-power is a limited resource. This was proven by Roy Baumeister, who was educated at Princeton University. He conducted a study where he placed two groups of people in a room filled with the aroma of fresh-baked cookies. He then put, on the table in the middle of the room, two plates, one with cookies and the other with radishes. Some subjects were asked to sample the cookies but not touch the radishes, while others were asked to eat the radishes, and leave the cookies. Afterward, each group was given 30 minutes to complete a problematic geometric puzzle. The results startles Baumeister and his colleagues. They repeatedly discovered that the people who ate radishes, exercising their will power to not have the cookies, gave up on the puzzle after about eight minutes. While the cookie-eaters persisted for nearly nineteen minutes, over twice as long. Drawing on one's willpower to resist the cookies seems to drained the subjects. This is why we all fail at our diet, new workout plans, and so much more. However, we no longer have that luxury as we are on your journey of Becoming A Bestseller. How do we resolve this?

1. **Commit to your word** — Tell your partner, your children, or someone you deeply respect and do not want to let down, that you are committed to finishing this book in 60 days.

2. **Social announcement** — Leverage your social network. Announce on your social platforms that you are going to post an updated word count each day. Make a quick video asking your friends and family to hold you accountable. The extra influence will drive your success.

3. **Partner or Coach** — We here at BABS have created a private Facebook group. Reach out and request an accountability partner. Commit to updating each other every day. If you want to truly level up and work with someone who has already been through the process, who is a proven bestseller, reach out directly to us at coaching@becomingabestseller. com

4. **Outlay funds and a Deadline** — Put your hard-earned money on the line. Purchase a marketing program and set the launch date. This will force you to hit milestones in advance.

5. **Make It Hurt** — I have been coaching clients on how to retire for over a decade. When we have a large, seeming unattainable goal, we always put a painful

cost for not completing it. Clients have created punishments for failing to be their word which have varied, but have included;

   a. Selling his Harley Davidson and giving all the funds directly to Hillary Clinton

   b. Taking the $10,000 of funds and giving them to the National Rifle Association

   c. Shaving her entire head

   d. Deleting all of his beloved photographs that were not of his family

   e. Getting a tattoo that says "I AM a LIAR"

Again these were all their choice; however, when making yours, make sure it is one that you will not break.

6. **Make it a competition.** Get a group of friends together and throw funds into a pot. Nothing extravagant, let's say $100. We do this with both of our Guaranteed Bestseller offerings. The entry level is where we bring together roughly 100 aspiring authors and have them join in as co-authors, guaranteeing Amazon Bestseller Status. They all throw in $50 and the winner takes all, plus becomes a bestseller. With our higher-level offering, we bring together eight chosen authors and I work directly with them creating a book that we guarantee to become a Wall Street Journal Bestseller. For that, the pot is quite a bit larger, however for you, start with something you and your accountability group can all agree on. It could be anything, but make it worth winning. A group of our aspiring authors chose a simple, but ridiculous trophy. The winner got to keep it and it became a real sense of pride for these guys.

NEXT STEPS

Becoming Accountable. Make it fun. Make it public. Be your word.

- Go to becomingabestseller.com and either create a free account or log in to your existing Path to Publish
- Take a moment and dig deep down and face your limiting beliefs. Write down your fears and turn them into fuel.
- Find an accountability group or partner and set some definitive goals. Then have fun building the reward. Make sure it is something you both really want.
- Now that you have clarity on your fears, goal, and rewards, tell everyone anywhere you can!

Again, it is important you take the time you need for your process and your book. Sure, I became a bestseller in 60 days, others have done it in less. Still others take longer. It is not about them or me, it is about you, what you want and the support you need.

YOUR BOOK'S TRUE HERO AND WHY THEY ARE THE ONLY ONE THAT CAN SAVE YOU

We live in a time of abundant heroes. We have Ironman, The Hulk, Superman, John Snow, Luke Skywalker, Harry Potter, and the list goes on and on. Are they the heroes? Not really, they are not real. The real heroes are Stan Lee, George R. R. Martin, George Lucas, and J. K. Rowling. The people who brought us into their worlds. THEIR WORLDS. It is important to understand that this is your world, your voice, and your dream. Sure, you could hire a ghost writer to write your entire book, and we know people who have. However, it will never be the same unless it is your voice. Only you can step up and write this book to the level and standard of your dreams. IF you don't, it will be lost forever. For many authors that is a motivating thought:

Imagine, if you will, being on your death bed —
and standing around your bed — the ghosts of
the ideas, the dreams, the abilities, the talents
given to you by life.

35

And that you for whatever reason, you never acted on those ideas, you never pursued that dream, you never used those talents, we never saw your leadership, you never used your voice, you never wrote that book.

And there they are standing around your bed looking at you with large angry eyes saying we came to you, and only you could have given us life! Now we must die with you forever.

The question is — if you die today what ideas, what dreams, what abilities, what talents, what gifts, would die with you?[8]

— Les Brown

Now there is a huge difference between a writer and an author. To make this easier, we will use me as an example. I am not a writer, in fact that is the main reason I am working on this book with Christine. If not for her, this book would be a ball of spelling, grammar, and lord knows what else. It would be simply unreadable. Every day, I write my portion, brain dump ideas onto a word document and she fixes it so it is fit for human consumption. All of this while she is writing and working on other things. That is her talent, I have mine. However calling me a writer is an insult to anyone who has ever written anything on any piece of paper: EVER! I am an author, and there are two types, according to George R. R. Martin:

"I think there are two types of writers, the archi-tects and the gardeners. The architects plan everything ahead of time, like an architect building a house. They know how many rooms are going to be in the house, what kind of roof they're going to have, where the wires are going to run, what kind of plumbing there's going to be. They have the whole thing designed and blueprinted out before they even nail the first board up. The gardeners dig a hole, drop in a seed and water it. They kind of know what seed it is, they know if they planted a fantasy seed or a mystery seed or whatever. But as the plant comes up and they water it, they don't know how many branches it's going to have, they find out as it grows."[9]

— George R.R. Martin

So which one do you think George is? The creator of the entire 5-book series with over five thousand pages?

"And I'm much more a gardener than an architect."[10]

— George R.R. Martin

Surprised?

Remember there is no right or wrong. It is, however, critical that you know exactly who you are and what your strengths are. When speaking, I am constantly asked if I wrote a book in nine days. The short answer is yes. The longer answer is technically fourteen days, but I was coaching, traveling, and had writer's block for two of them. Sounds crazy right? Nope, and the Path to Publish, along with FREE Facebook group at becomingabestseller.com, will help you do the same. So how did I do it?

You have already started on the first steps on the Path to Publish, the same that made me a bestseller. You know your purpose, your audience, and your fears. We next have to discover your strengths and weaknesses. For me it is spelling, grammar, proper structure, tense, run-on sentences and....

It is embarrassing how poor my technical writing ability is, so I outsourced it to my assistant. Even though it is her THIRD language, she is still light years better then I will ever be. So, I would write five to twenty thousand words during the day, and she would edit it. The knowledge that she was behind me, supporting me without judgment, was the only reason I could produce so much content in such a short time. Every morning, at 9 AM, we would jump on skype and talk about the previous section. She would ask me questions, show me where the thoughts failed to materialize, and off I would go. If I were to worry about grammar, and all the other weaknesses I have, not a single paragraph would ever have been written.

And how much did this cost me?
$4/hour

A few things to get out of the way before we go any further.

1.   No, I am not sharing Christine.
2.   Yes, she is real, amazing and I am blessed to have her.
3.   Again, NO, I am not sharing Christine.
4.   Finally, NO, I am not sharing Christine.

How do you get your own Christine? Upwork.com

Upwork, is an international freelancing platform where you can connect remotely to businesses and independent professionals from around the world. Each is reviewed and rated, just like a product at Amazon.com. Christine started as my VA, virtual assistant, and now is mission critical to my entire success. The process is relatively simple. You go online to upwork.com, search for what you need, and then sort by reviews. In our course, Becoming a Bestseller, we created a detailed walkthrough and even showed a few of my active jobs and how we search for our freelancers. Sure, there are other sites out there, like Fiverr.com, but we have had the best results with Upwork.

There is, of course, the ability to hire a ghost writer or a dedicated team over at authorsunite.net. They have years of experience and the ability to help you in becoming a best-seller so well, that my team has partnered with them.

NEXT STEPS

Focus on what will make you unstoppable.

- Go to becomingabestseller.com and either create a free account or log in to your existing Path to Publish
- Time for a list:
  - What you are good at
  - What you are horrific at
  - What you are good at but don't want to do
  - What things only you can do
  - What you are willing to pay someone else to do.
- Review your list and post a job on whichever freelancing site you want.
- Test your freelancer on a few minor things. See if you two work well together.
- Reach out to the group at the Becoming a Bestseller Facebook group (BABS) and ask if anyone has resources they want to share.

THE IDEA

THAT

LAUNCHES

IT ALL

On this point of our *Path to Publish*, we have our methods, leveraged points, and even a few hacks. Yet what on earth are you going write about? How do you know what, out of all the ideas you have, that you are going to push forward with to achieve your purpose and dream? The method below is proven to help you narrow it down. At the end of this section, you are one step closer to Becoming a Bestseller.

GETTING STARTED:

Step 1:	List ten things you enjoy talking about.
	One of our clients adores the spoken word of faith. However, he can talk endlessly about photography, video production, and sales. In his case, we had him write down all three.
Step 2:	Now let's rank them by what you enjoy the most. 1-10, highest to lowest.
Step 3:	Now cut the list in half to five. Remember we are not getting rid of the other ideas, we are just choosing your FIRST book.
Step 4:	With the remaining five; which ones will help you serve your purpose and goal? Cut out the rest.
	For example, I love scuba diving, however I coach entrepreneurs on how to retire. Which one would you like me to write about? It is always critical to give your audience what they want, not what you want.

Step 5: Now look at what is remaining; could you write a book about them? In other words, if you were forced to talk about this topic, without any warning, to a classroom full of people, would you:

    1.   Have enough information to share?

    2.   Enjoy sharing it?

    3.   Want to speak to the people in the class after, one on one?

Step 6: Cross out all the "No(s)"

Step 7: For the remaining "Yes(s)", what value can your personal voice bring to this topic? Can you deliver that to the world?

Step 8: How can you monetize this:

    1.   Book sales

    2.   Courses

    3.   Speaking

    4.   Subscriptions

    5.   Retreats

    6.   Other opportunities

Step 9: Narrow your list down to only two options

Step 10: Stop deciding on if you are going to do one OR the other. It is not about that. It is about which one are you going to do first?

*** Notice that monetization is LAST not FIRST ***

SALES: WHERE OTHERS **FAIL**, AND WHY YOU WON'T.

THE ONLY RULE IN SALES

If there is only one thing you remember from this entire book, please make it be this:

*It is not what you **sell**. It is what you **solve**.*

Your audience is your customer and if we are not eliminating their real pain we are failing. If we are talking about how amazing we are, and how great our product is, we will fail. Let's take two radar detector salesmen as an example.

Salesman one pitch: This is the greatest radar detector in the world. It is made of space-age turtle plastic. It uses our proprietary 4533 GHz radar band technology, developed by scientists from NASA. It can detect an officer's radar gun a quarter mile before any of our competition. It comes with a ninety-day warranty.

Salesman two pitch: We think this is the best radar detector on the market. So much so that we guarantee you will not get a speeding ticket. However, if you do, we will pay for it.

Who do you buy from?

WHAT PEOPLE BUY

Understanding what people are really buying goes against everything we have been taught. We are taught that people buy products and services. They don't.

People do not buy products and services. They do buy stories, identities, and ways away from pain. When a person buys a BMW, are they buying a car? Or are they buying the identity, the luxury, and the reaction of the people they will drive by? When someone shops at Wholefoods vs their local supermarket, what are they buying? Food? Or are they looking for the most nutritious food source, wrapped in an upscale environment? What about the people that are buying from Trader Joes? Food is food, right? Organic is organic? Yet one bag of apples cost twice as much at Wholefoods as it does at Trader Joes. How about a fake purse vs a real purse? For the price of a real purse you could buy a hundred fake purses and they could fail every three months, but people still buy the real one. Is the authentic one that much better? Better, yes. A hundred times better, no. Sadly, and heartbreakingly, more people are driven by a simple mindset:

1. Am I enough?
2. If I am enough, maybe I will be worthy of love.

WHO ARE THEY, AND DO YOU WANT TO SELL TO THEM?

Early on in everyone's professional career, all we want to do is focus on sales. In time that changes. However, the focus is to narrow down your target audience because it will dynamically change how you interact with them. Unlocking the following will help you know exactly what they want, and position yourself as the only way to get it.

1. WHERE ARE THEY?

This concept is commonly known as the "watering hole". It simply breaks down your audience into persona and characters. Imagine you are wearing a tux and are at The White House. Now imagine you are in your bathing suit and you are coasting down a river in a tub with a drink in your hand. Are you using the same language? Are your friends? Do the people on the river have different wants and needs than the ones in The White House? Do they use different language? Of course they do. Knowing where your audience is congregating is critical. What blogs are they reading? What websites, podcasts, magazines, music, television shows, and movies are they watching?

2. WHAT LANGUAGE ARE THEY USING?

This is not just about languages and dialects. This is about rapport. We, as humans, trust people that we like and we like people who are similar to us. If you are around a group of Star Wars Fans at a show and you start talking about Star Trek, you just break rapport. People who are in their 20s use very different language than people in their 30s. Just how it is. Use the language in your sales copy and material that mirrors the language your audience is comfortable using and seeing on a daily basis.

3. WHO DO THEY TRUST ALREADY?

Ever wonder why some famous sports player is selling that drink? Or those shoes? People in the '90s thought if they bought Michael Jordan's shoes, we would somehow gain some hidden talent. The cloth and plastic on our feet would allow me to dunk when we were thirteen. Or that somehow, by wearing the same watch as a special forces Navy SEAL, we would become super heroes like them. Sadly it never works. Yet we keep buying it over and over and over and over and... ok you get the point. This is why endorsements are such a huge business. Again, it is not about right or wrong, it is about reality. People buy from people they trust. Leveraging relationships is critical to obtaining the launch you need for your book.

4. WHAT PAIN ARE THEY IN?

If you can position your product or service and the key solution to helping them break free from the pain and anxiety that is keeping them up at night, you win. It is that simple. However, you must understand their pain on a deep level. What words do they use to describe it? How is it affecting their lives? Their loved ones' lives? Building your marketing material around this will level up your material against your competition.

5. WHAT BRANDS ARE THEY BUYING ALREADY?

Again this goes towards the rapport concept. If someone is already buying Nike, they are used to a certain language, tone and cadence to their marketing material. Leverage those billions of dollars and decades of exposure. Finding a way to align with that similar message is a simple access point to introduce your book to your audience.

The more you know about your audience, what they choose to be open to, and how they interact with each other, the easier your launch will be.

THE DEFINITIVE GUIDE TO
REACHING YOUR GOALS

A dear friend and former client is a combat veteran for the legendary Mossad, which is a part of The Institute for Intelligence and Special Operations. When he started out as a client, I was honored to be in support of him while he was finding a new normal through PTSD (Post Traumatic Stress Disorder). Throughout more battle stories and lost friends than I care to remember, there was a moment where a simple question arose: "How were you so successful? How are you alive?" He responded in Hebrew, and then translated it as:

"Let your last move be your first decision"

— Mossad Sniper

He went on to explain that clarity of purpose is critical to success and that one cannot hit the targets in life, if they have not clearly defined them. His further explanation has helped myself and other clients over the years to reach dreams they once thought impossible. He then broke the process down as follows:

Step 1:	What do you think you really want?
	Write down the three things that you really want.

Step 2:	Why do you want it?
	Is it leverage and significance? Is it income? Or is it both?
	If it is business growth, then it is less about measuring sales that make you a bestseller and more about measuring the impact to your bottom line. Books can dramatically change your income stream in many ways:

SERVICES:

i. Email Subscribers

Your audience will grow as your exposure increases. Later we will teach you about funnels, growth metrics, and leveraging your lists.

ii. Coaching clients

Establishing yourself as the expert in any field will bring people wanting to learn and benefit from your expertise. Please note: do not coach unless you are willing to be selflessly in service to others.

iii. Consulting Clients

If your service is not in a coaching format, your book will do wonders in launching you service to your new client base. One of our recent clients established himself as a video expert for shooting YouTube videos and his business tripled in the first 45 days.

iv. Membership Programs

People want access to not only your materials, but to the successful and recognized author. Tying this access to a membership portal where they can work together with like-minded people is a proven profit model.

PRODUCTS:

v. Books alone

The key is not selling a single book, but building up a series of books. Think of the "Dummies" series that taught people how to do complex tasks in layman's terms. THINK SERIES NOT SINGLE

vi. Goods

When it comes to leveraging your bestseller status for increasing the sales of your goods, a book alone is not enough. We can make you #1 on every list, however if your product fails to provide value, it does not matter. Remember, products, just like services, must provide value by answering the following three things:

1. Is it clear what you are offering?
2. How exactly will it make your customer's life better?
3. What specifically do they need to bring it into their lives

Step 3:   What are you willing to sacrifice?
Will you sacrifice sleep? Relationships? Food? Comfort? Vacations? Try and push the examples to the extreme and then filter through those extremes. Becoming a bestseller is a commitment of time, energy, and resources. The authors that succeed are far beyond want, but are willing to go those few extra steps on the Path to Publish to obtain their dreams.

THE PERFECT PLAN

As we move forward into the execution phase of actually writing your bestseller, our Path to Publish will play a critical role. Because of it, we know what the purpose of the book is. We have clearly defined the products or services we are going to support with it. Finally we have tackled fear and eliminated some limiting beliefs. The rest of the book is going to start leaving concepts and start driving towards execution. With all successful ventures, we must define our end result with a plan.

SIZE MATTERS — HOW BIG DO YOU WANT TO GET?

This all depends on your network, your net worth, and your previous experience. For me, I leveraged and partnered with Authors Unite (authorsunite.net) in order to accomplish my goals. One of the first questions they ask was: *"Which list do you want to hit?"*

Much like all of us, my reaction was simple and at the time, naive: "All of them."

Having made over 700 bestsellers, they were ready and prepared for that response. Then the breakdown of bestsellers by list started:

Want to be an Amazon bestseller:	Plan your launch with a lot of sales in one day
Want to be an WSJ/ USA Today bestseller:	Plan your launch with a lot of sales across a solid week
Want to be an NYT bestseller:	Plan a huge launch, a full marketing budget, mid six-figure budget, and a six-month roll out.

This was jarring the first time, because the dream of NYT now felt so far away. The people at AU quickly had a solution for that. The New York Times bestseller list has changed over the recent months. It is no longer based on sales, but on option and reach. AU expressed they could make it happen, but probably not on your first book. One needs success in a self-published launch to be picked up by any of the major publishing houses, and then a launch can be attempted. As you can tell, this is a much longer process.

HOW THICK IS IT?

As you start writing your book, it is critical that you fully understand your capacity early on. Can you write 500 words a day? A 1000? Are you a writing machine and can produce 20,000? It is important to know that most books are roughly 60,000 words. With that goal of 60,000 words and if we take our previous list, that the average person can do 1000 words a day, that means 30k is produced in a month, or 60k words in two months. Again, some people do 10k words in a sitting, some do 60k in a weekend, and knowing your abilities as a writer is key.

Once you have your goal in place, do the math. Let's say you want 60,000 words and you want it done in 90 days; the math is not 60,000 divided by 90. You need to be prepared for edits, and roughly 10% of your work to be eliminated during that process. On top of that, there is writer's block and days where no matter what you create, it comes out as unusable. Just happens even to the best of us. So, the formula might look something like this:

Goal	60,000 words
10% Purge	6,000 words
Total	66,000 words
Number of days	90 days
10% loss	9 days
New number of days	81 days
New totals	66,000 words / 81 days = 815 words a day

Remember that is just time to write, we have not gotten into editing which normally takes two weeks to a month. However, you will soon learn the plan and process we use in Becoming a Bestseller. One that reduces time and costs to almost zero. And the final part we must not forget is having systems in place to capture leads. Don't worry, we are sharing some of our most proven templates and plans at becomingabestseller.com.

NEXT STEPS

Leverage the market to your needs.

- Go to becomingabestseller.com and either create a free account or log in to your existing Path to Publish
- Fill out the Audience Awareness Section
  - Where are they?
  - What language are they using?
  - Who do they trust already?
  - What pain are they in?
  - What brands are they buying already?
- Once you have a clear picture of your audience, read what they are reading. Try and review the books they are currently buying. Look at the covers, the language, and the materials they are already open and committed to.
- Get things really quiet and pull out the Path to Publish and focus on the goals section. Be honest with what YOU want. Not what your friends, family, or ego wants. What are you willing to sacrifice? What are you willing to build your future around? If you are serious about truly ensuring your book launch produces the leverage, passive income, and unlocks the doors holding you back from your dreams, then reach out to us at coaching@becomingabestseller.com
- Reach out to the group at the Becoming a Bestseller Facebook group (BABS) and discover who else is working on the same audience. Share notes and work together. The market is large enough to serve us all, especially with high value content.

NOTES

THE

ROADBLOCKS

THAT STOP

ALL AUTHORS,

AND HOW

TO SMASH

THEM

"I learned that courage was not the absence of fear, but the triumph over it. The brave man is not he who does not feel afraid, but he who conquers that fear."[11]

—Nelson Mandela

We have spoken about fear earlier. Now you are going to discover that there are 6 ways to eliminate fear, that are used by the ultra-successful. Before we start, it is critical to remember that fear is not real. It is a product of thoughts you create. Do not misunderstand me. Danger is very real. But fear is a choice.

Fear   Face Everything and Rise
           Fuck Everything and Run

Tool #1:
Awareness

This fear is real. It will happen...it is not in your imagination. Some people are going to love your book. Others are going to hate it:

Here are some real reviews:

"It is really confusing and weird and dumb."

"Not worth the Money!"

"Much Ado About Nothing."

Which book was this?

Harry Potter and The Sorcerer's Stone, by J.K. Rowling. A book with over thirty-five thousand positive reviews on Amazon. Still people simply did not like it.

We can all hope that our books are as well received. However even with that, there are some who simply will not like your book. It is one of the few guarantees in life. Having that level of awareness allows you to prepare for the inevitable. It is much like getting on the highway to head home at five o'clock and being upset that there is traffic. Of course there is traffic! So either leave earlier or later. If that is not an option, take that awareness, and make sure you have your favorite music in the car for your ride home.

Knowing that you will have bad reviews must not stop you; everyone gets them.

**Tool #2:
Indifference**

There will be a large group of people who will not like your book. Some will be friends; others will be family. You book will meet the needs of one audience and push away another. If you make a book on opera, some will hate it. If you make a book on politics, some will hate it while others will think it is perfect. Ever watch the show Game of Thrones? I love the show to the point of addiction and daily debates; hate the books. Sadly George R. R. Martin learned about my personal dislike for his books and entered a deep bout of depression. Wrong! People in your real life don't like you, and you don't like some people as well. Did anyone die? Did the author? Did you? NO, and you won't, so let it go and move on.

**Tool #3:
Nothing is final**

We are taught that when you finish your book and put it out into the world, it is a final product. Shockingly this is incorrect. You can and will edit your book even after it is edited and published. We all do. They are called revisions. Better yet, most of the errors and issues will be discover for you. In fact, people will pay for your books and then send you emails telling you where the issues are. There will be mistakes no matter how many editors, and some of your readers will help point errors out, especially your haters. Haters are nothing more than a free group of editors; got to love them.

Tool #4: **Honor your truth**	Your book will make a stand, will declare a truth, and tell a story. A story most people have never heard and one that will, hopefully, make them think in a new and unique way. People will revolt against that, as did George Washington and our forefathers. When they came together, do you think they were worried about what would and wouldn't upset the monarch? When Tim Ferris wrote his book The Four-Hour Work Week, was he worried that every employer on the plane would be upset that their staff would want to quit the next day? Of course not. Honor your truth above anyone else and at the end of the day the person looking back in the mirror will honor you.
Tool #5: **It is your** **opportunity**	For the first time in most of our lives, our book is a chance to tell the world who we really are. In school we had to dress a certain way, take certain classes, and sit in specific seat. That continued with work when we had to show up at a certain time, do the work the way they wanted us to, and listen to their rules. Not here. Not with your book. Remember it is not just about the book, it is about the branding, the leverage, and the fact that it is just one of many steps toward a path of your creation and the life you desire.

Tool #6:
Fear is Fuel

In Who Changes Everything, I wrote a detailed process of how the entrepreneurs that I coach leveraged their fear as a fuel source. One of my clients would wake up with panic attacks. She was unsure what her fate would be and how to pay for her kid' studies. We worked on her plan, broke it out in detail and were struggling with the time and energy needed to implement it. One extremely early morning, she woke up and called in pure panic. She expressed how the fear was overwhelming, that she did not know when she would find the time and energy to move forward. She expressed that she was always tired and things were never quiet enough. I asked her if she was tired at that moment, and if she could go to bed. She barked at me expressing that she was not tired and was freaking out. To this I simply replied, "So you are not tired, have tons of energy, and the kids are asleep?" She immediately realized that her fear had become the fuel source that woke her up early and was fueling the fire to her success, be it not on her schedule. From that point forward, whenever she stopped calling these moments panic attacks and renamed them go time, she would wake up, with tons of fear, harness it as a fuel source and burn through it trying to accomplish a task. At times it was successful, sometimes it just meant that she cleaned the whole house. Other times it would last hours, sometimes minutes. The end result was a six-figure residual income and time to finally start dating. She had harnessed her fear, and so can you.

MAKING YOUR ENVIRONMENT
WORK FOR YOU

What is the number one reason people do not finish their books? Their environment.

Once they launch beyond their fears, and leverage that untapped fuel source, they sit down to write. But wait, what about food, oh and that thing I forgot to do, and oh look there is a bird outside, and so on. Your environment must serve you beyond just being your place to type.

Step 1:
Take back
the Tech

Turn off your phone and mobile devices if possible. If it is not, put them into do not disturb mode and add your critical people to VIP status. Doing this will allow their messages to come in, but nothing else. Therefore, if it is an emergency, the call or message comes through.

Then turn off all notifications. This is a good idea regardless, however disabling the constant attention grabs from every app is vital to success. Try and do a week of no notifications and see how much more productive you are. Yes, this also includes reminders.

Now it comes to your computer or laptop. This is easier; close all other programs and disable the internet. It is amazing how useless a computer feels when it no longer has access to the internet. You will also be amazed how much work you get done as well.

If it is within budget, get a pair of noise-canceling head phones. If those are not within the current budget, ear plugs work almost as well.

Step 2: Control your space

This starts with more of the accountability we spoke about. Before you write, announce it on social media, to your family, and take the dog out for a walk. Try to eliminate any and all other excuses/outs we all give each other when there is a critical task to accomplish.

Once you are done, go to your space and lock the door. I had an old spare laptop that barely did anything but my word processing software. It had no other apps on it, and I bought a tiny desk that was more of a side table than a desk. There were no drawers and just enough room for a pad of paper and a glass of water. The jug of water that I kept with me while writing had to be on the floor, as there was no space on the desk.

Everyone knew that unless the house was on fire or there was a real medical emergency, I was not to be bothered.

Sound — is all about personal preference. Some love silence and will even obtain a set of noise-canceling headphones or ear plugs. While others love background noise and play instrumental music. A large number of our authors use: Brain.FM

Mood — are you a dark room type of person? What about candles or incense? I am not, I am a vacuum and CDO (OCD in the right order) type of guy. I always vacuumed my writing area before I started and wiped down my desk, that way It was clean and ready to go.

Food comes down to two words: MEAL PREP! We can easily get distracted by the need to eat. Our mind will tell us all of the things we MUST do instead of writing. Having your meals, snack, and drinks ready to go will allow you to push beyond the distractions.

Step 3: Mental Mastery

It is key to remember the first 10 minutes are the most difficult, and your mind will try and distract you. We all have what is known as the monkey mind. It will want to jump around telling us that there are other things to do, other things that must be handled, and urgent games to play. So let it. Set a timer of 15 minutes and rock through the following tasks:

1. Open your email and answer the urgent emails.
2. Quickly check in on the news, and social media.
3. To-do lists — Take out a piece of paper and write down everything that you need to do.
4. Once that is all done, use the rest room.
5. Grab some water.
6. And review the purpose of your book. Where are you going once it is done and why are you writing it?
7. Then close everything down and get to work

There are times as an author you will be in flow, while other times you will be a mess. Don't fight through the mess. The result will be poor copy and subpar work. There were many times when writing my bestseller, that my mind needed a break. So, I would get up, grab my iPhone, and play a game on the couch. Just something mindless and relaxing. This would allow my body to breathe, mind to stretch, and hands to relax. Whenever the break was done, I would immediately feel recharged and headed back into work.

FEAR BECOMES FUN

"It's kind of fun to do the impossible."[12]

— Walt Disney

As with so many things in life, the only ones we enjoy doing are the ones that are fun. Writing a book is one of those things. One that will live far beyond you, and will end up in the hands of your descendants. To lessen that burden, let's review a few ways to ease the pressure and make this fun.

REMOVE EXPECTATIONS

Your book is going to suck and it is going to be amazing. Will it change the world? Probably not. Will it change your life? Probably. So every time you sit down to write, just relax and try to enjoy. You will remember the process far more than you will remember the book.

KNOW YOUR STRENGTHS AND WEAKNESSES

As we have already determined, I cannot spell, write or anything remotely that looks like a book. What I can do is toss a great deal of information at a page and go back after to clean it up. That is my strength, and as we have discussed before, I outsource my weaknesses. Spend the time jotting down what you are good at, and what you are horrible at. Outsource anything that will slow you down. It is why we have partnered up with Authors Unite and support their done for you program.

MAKE A MESS

Don't be so organized. So many writers try and try and write it in order. We are not building a house, we are writing a book. The parts are interchangeable, and you will modify them dozens of times. Some of us will write titles, subtitles, trying to be so professional out of the gate. That works for them; my mind would explode if I tried that. Try to recall the conversation George R. R. Martin shared with us about being an architect or a farmer. Make this a must like when you were a child, just go with it and you will discover your own path.

THERE IS NO ORDER

First get the material out of your head and we will review brain dumps soon. Then read over what you wrote, then write more. You can organize it later. When we were kids we would play with Legos. First step was to pour them out on the floor and build as you go. As we built, the piece would help our imagination build what was in our mind. Same is true for your bestseller. As we have reviewed, there are things to keep in mind:

1. Think of who your audience is.
2. Write as if you were speaking to them, literally as you speak.
3. What do they want?
4. Are they in pain?
5. What are their dreams?
6. How are you trying to make them feel?

CHERISH THE MOMENT

In other words: Gratitude. I spent 8 years working in a hospice watching people die. Trust me, they would love to have the woes of writing a book. Being grateful is the only scientifically proven direct hack to our minds. You are writing a book! I mean holy crap! You are writing a book! A book that can change everything. You are alive in this moment and have the luxury to sit down and share your voice with the world. There is tremendous beauty in that moment.

THERE IS NO PERFECT

Let Go of perfect. There is no perfect. You are going to write a lot of crap, some of it you won't use at all. That is ok. We all do. Just remember there is no perfect. Even better, soon you will order your first copy to review, which is called a proof. Just like the rest of us, there will be new errors, second-guessing logo choices and so much more! It is ok, it is supposed to happen.

MAKE IT A GAME

Set a goal, and then try to beat it. Compete with your accountability partner and if you don't have one, go to our Facebook group at becomingabestseller.com and reach out for one. Once you meet each milestone, give yourself a reward. Massages, great meals, or simply seeing a movie are all ways that you can make the process fun.

BRAIN DUMP

Untangling all of the information that is flooding your mind is critical and you MUST NOT SKIP THIS STEP. We have worked with over 700 authors who have become bestsellers and they all pull back to this as being the moment where it all started to make sense.

So, what exactly is a brain dump? In its simplest form, a brain dump is the process of writing down all the contents, thoughts, and ideas onto a single piece of paper. Imagine your mind was a handbag; this would be the process of emptying it onto a table. Out come your ideas, nagging thoughts, fears, doubts, unfinished concepts, and everything else that will ultimately become your bestseller. For most of us, a single paper is not enough. This is why I use a Post-it Super Sticky Easel Pad that is 25×30 Inches and comes with 30 Sheets. Peeling them off and placing them all over the walls allows me to finally think and see the concept in one place. While you are brain dumping, just let it flow and whatever comes out, comes out. During one of my first attempts, it turned into a to-do list for work at the house. Not 100% applicable to my book, but it freed up my mind, none the less.

HOW TO BRAIN DUMP

1. Get a big sheet of paper, or multiple pieces of paper, or a white board, or a chalk board, or a wall, a poster board, or a friend's back...or even your dog. Ok the last two might be too much, however we need a huge area to just go through your ideas.
2. Just start writing, there is no rhyme or reason. No order or plan, just get it all out.
3. Once the ideas are out, try and see how they connect to each other.
4. Taking the time to record yourself while you are writing will allow you to capture some ideas that come out faster than you can write. Going back and reviewing the audio or video helps a great deal.
5. Understand that this will take about 2 hours; at the end your will have the beginning of your bestseller.
6. Accept that your entire ideal book will not be fully fleshed out in this process. More will come later, however. List every topic you can think of, every story line — Don't worry if it is going to stay or not... just write it down. Some we will keep, some will turn into other things...some will be gold.
7. DO NOT Skip this step!

ORGANIZING YOUR FUTURE

There it is. Your masterpiece, scattered across the debris field of the mental purge, covering multiple pieces of paper. At this point you are probably starting to feel either relaxed or overwhelmed. Just breathe, it is in there, and remember the chant of the entire process:

Perfection is the enemy of execution.

We now need to organize it into a layout and format. Something that makes sense and is clear. This is normally when we turn to outlines. Yet which to choose? There are so many different choices on which outline works best. Just the names are overwhelming: skeletal, sketchbook, snowflake, novel, reverse, and so many more. Having worked with so many authors, we have discovered the best one: the one that you actually do.

Starting to see a pattern here of what works? Becoming a bestseller is a simple process that most have made far too complicated for their own good. It is much like the old expression: How do you eat an elephant? One bite at a time.

The outline process we use the most is simple, and it starts with looking at the brain dump. Ok so you have thrown up on a piece of paper; now it is time to make some sort of sense of it all. For most authors, the simple brain dump has already changed the shape of your book. Some of the book has changed, some has been dropped off all together, and even more ideas have been inspired. Now it is time to choose our gold and save some for the other books we will create.

STEPS:

1. Label the ideas that you think you could write a whole chapter or at least 3,000+ words on.

2. The remaining ones that do not stand on their own, start putting them together to form a chapter.

3. Pieces can become topics, topics can become sections, sections can become chapters, and chapters become books.

4. Now label the ones that will not be in the book. Write them down on another piece of paper and store them away. Protect them for your next bestseller.

5. Do not try to organize them yet. Just pick one and start to write. Remember we are writing everything as separate chapters. It just makes it easier.

6. Remember, after you have written your chapter, then you write your introduction and your conclusion. Not before.

7. Don't worry about the order; as you write, that will come naturally.

Wait, that does not sound like an outline at all! That just sounds like writing. You are correct. We are just about flow; the organization will come in time. Too many authors write an outline and then think they must stick to it like a self-imposed prison. Outlines are much like a map. Sure, there are direct routes, but there are side streets and rest stops as well.

NEXT STEPS

Prepare your writing workspace.

- Go to becomingabestseller.com and either create a free account or log in to your existing Path to Publish.
- Create a checklist that should include all the necessary things that you need to do before you start writing:
    o Are you in a quiet room?
    o Do you have your tech in a separate room?
    o Have you set the mood for your writing space?
    o Have you created an outline for your manuscript?
    o Have you mind-mapped all the information in your head on a piece of paper?
- If you are facing problems in creating your outline or mind-mapping, reach out to us at coaching@becomingabestseller.com and we are more than willing to help you with it.

NOTES

WRITING

THAT

MAKES

YOU A

BESTSELLER

ow can seven simple letters take down so many aspiring authors? Worse yet, when they discover the writing is the easy part, they freak out. Much like I am guessing you are doing now, just please remember to breathe. Writing is the enjoyable part. Then comes the editing, proofreading, reedits, design, more edits, and of course finally, even more edits. Don't worry, we will share the ways to outsource all of the unpleasant stuff. Time to answer a simple question: What is writing about? Your vision? Your message to the world? Your artistic, untapped potential? If you want to become a bestseller, the answer is: NO.

When writing a bestseller, your writing must first go through your filter of purpose. Remember from your Path to Publish we had you write down your purpose? It is back, as is you targeted audience. A bestseller is about sales, plain and simple. Sales is about very specific things:

1. It is not about you. It is about your audience.
2. It is not about what you sell. It is about what you solve.
3. You must position yourself as the only person who can solve the issue for your audience.
4. They are the most important then, and giving them immediate actionable items provides value.

Remember, people are not buying goods or services. They are buying stories, identities, and ways out of pain. Constantly use their language and keep it as simple as possible.

To sell more, become a P.A.S.T.O.R.

For most of us, we associate the term "pastor" with the preacher at church or some other religious institution. However for our needs, we are not suggesting any religious implications. Instead P.A.S.T.O.R. is also an acronym for the hidden secret to successful writing.

"P" is for PROBLEM/PAIN

Everything starts with the problem that you are solving or the pain you are eliminating. In order for your audience to relate to you, they must understand that you feel what they are going through in the simplest, most effective way possible. Psychology teaches us that if this is done, if your audience truly thinks you understand them, they instinctively trust in your answer. This is why social proof is so important. There are hundreds or thousands of people who want to share with you the process of becoming a bestseller. However, we here at BABS have successfully helped hundreds of authors reach their goals, along with Charles being a WSJ Bestseller himself. As the great copywriting legend Robert Collier said, you have to "join the conversation that is already taking place in the reader's mind."

"A" is for AMPLIFY

Now it is time to increase the consequences of failing to resolve their problem. You are asking your audience to part with their hard-earned cash. To do that you must show them what life looks like if they don't. Without this they will never be motivated to buy your product or invest in your service. Simply put: How is it currently affecting them not to solve this problem in their lives? What is it costing them to continually fail to solve this problem?

"S" is for SOLUTION

Once the problem is identified, and then amplified, your audience will be searching for a way free from the pain. They now know the detailed consequences of not solving this problem. It is time to rescue them and share how they can resolve the issue in THREE easy steps. It must be simple at all times. This is not the time to cover them in details. Break it down for them in three sections: do this, then this, and achieve that. Period

"T" is for TRANSFORMATION and TESTIMONY

They now know the pain, they know the cost for not taking action, and finally have access to your solution. However, they still will not buy. You must show them the end before they will risk the journey. This is where proof of concept or service comes into play. If they read your book on working out, show pictures of the results. If your book is about becoming an amazing speaker, share stories of previous clients speaking at fortune 500 seminars. Think of every fitness program you have seen on TV, they always show you some before picture of an obese, out-of-shape person who looks far worse than you do. Then immediately, a new picture of massive transformation shows how they now look like the cover of a fitness magazine. You must do this for your audience as well. Painting a picture of how amazing life will look once they have purchased your product or service is critical.

"O" is for OFFER

Now is the part where you get simple and specific, with copy that makes it clear what they receive. Something creative like "This is what is included" or "Here's Exactly What You Get.". Once you have declared this, you must immediately bring them back to their transformation or the dream you are selling them. This can be done by stating "Not only do you get two for the price of one, but you will never worry about backed up toilets again. Freeing yourself from that nagging mother-in-law once and for all."

"R" is for REQUEST

Your client is at the point of decision, however they will not take action unless you tell them exactly what to do. Welcome to the illusion of choice. Your customers must be told what do to over and over: "Click the button below, fill out the order form, and we will immediately ship your entire package to you. It will contain everything you need to get started." When it comes to your book, this is about tying in your product or service throughout the book.

As you look over your book, try and imagine the P.A.S.T.O.R. process weaving its way in and out for sections and chapters. You can always have your writing reflect that level of attention and intent. Remember, unless you are writing a passion project, you have a clear and focus goal in mind beyond the book.

RIDING THE WAVE

With all authors, we find a Writer's Flow, or a moment in time where your fingers simply can't keep up and the ideas stream out like water. This normally happens after 10 or so minutes of writing. And there are a few ways to get it started. Contrary to popular belief, it is not staring at a screen. You have to move. Dance. Walk around your room. Just don't do anything else. I listen to a ton of music; or if I got stuck, I would go grab food. There is a term in the military, movement is life. Sitting down and forcing it will only produce low-end and mediocre content. This why we have you write down a to-do list, have snacks on the standby, and chores already completed. This is also why we have your space clear and clean.

So, what causes writers block? Perfection! Perfection is the enemy of execution. Yet not for us; when we get stuck, we are going to refer to our outline, our brain dump. We are going to remember the purpose of our book, and that we will never be perfect. What we will not do is force it; to just type for the need of typing. Type something, even if it is bad, but it is close. From there you can go back and read I later and it will inspire you. DON'T FORCE IT. I lost over 15k words because I forced it when I was tired. I could tell, my readers could tell, as could my editing team. It was bad and cost me time. However, typing nonsense that just comes out, vague nonsense, sometimes helps.

The final secret weapon to writer's block: **STAY HYDRATED**.

Now that you are in flow, what do you do? Ride that wave until it crashes into the beach! Do not stop writing. One flow took me to over 22k words in a day. The next day...nothing. I could barely finish a sentence at first. Which was ok. Once you break flow, it is hard to get it back. Knowing this, I decided to work out and give my mind something else to do. Writer's flow will come back, but it is hard to predict. This is why no interruptions are critical. Yet they do happen and they knock you out of flow. Sadly, once you are knocked out, it is difficult to jump back in, if at all. Accept this as part of the process, just as we have accepted negative reviews and simply move forward.

TITLES THAT EXCITE YOUR READERS

Ever been to the supermarket and seen the trash magazines? The ones that talk about celebrity gossip, or outrageous news? How do they stay in business? I mean who buys those things? Millions of us do. Why? Because viral titles and shock value works. As does speaking directly to the pain and desires of your audience. No one knows this better than Tim Ferris of the Four-Hour Work Week fame and he mastered it by the time he wrote the Four-Hour Body. If you take a look at the Table of Contents (TOC) from this book, he left some amazing subtitles:

- Thinner, Bigger, Faster, Stronger? How to Use This Book
- Rules That Change the Rules: Everything Popular Is Wrong
- From Photos to Fear: Making Failure Impossible
- The Slow-Carb Diet I: How to Lose 20 Pounds in 30 Days Without Exercise
- Damage Control: Preventing Fat Gain When You Binge
- The Last Mile: Losing the Final 5-10 Pounds
- Six-Minute Abs: Two Exercises That Actually Work
- Happy Endings and Doubling Sperm Count
- Perfecting Sleep
- Reversing "Permanent" Injuries

And these are just the PG ones. We already know he is a master of titles: 4-Hour Body, 4-Hour Work Week, etc. We now have clear examples of great titles, but how can we make our own?

Welcome to End Result Titling. This type of titling for your book is all about telling the audience exactly what happens when they read the book. In the P.A.S.T.O.R. process we call this result and this was the final step.

Here are a few examples:

a. 4-hour Work Week
b. How to Win Friends and Influence People
c. Who Changes Everything
d. Money: Master the Game

Again, it is critical that you know the language your audience is speaking. Think of a dating site; one for 20-year-olds is going to use very different language than ones for 30-year-olds.

Where it is easy to conceptualize, it is more difficult to actually produce. So, how do you come up with it? Simple: Sticky pad time! Get out your large wall-sized Post-it notes and start searching on your topic. Look at any magazines. Any blog posts. Try and write down all of the most common words that your audience is being sold to. For example:

Men — Powerful, strong, cut, money, six pack.

Women — sexy, lose fat, fashion, ambition, stress, beauty and so forth.

Then take all of the most common words and try to come up with an end result. Try Stress Free Fat Loss. From there we need to talk about subtitles:

Subtitles do one thing above all else; they explain exactly what the reader is going to get.

4-Hour Work Week:
Escape 9-5, Live Anywhere, and Join the New Rich

The Power of Now:
The guide to Spiritual Enlightenment

Note: when choosing a title, try and search if the domain is available.

THE ROUGH DRAFT TO PERFECTION

The most common question I get about my book is:

"Did I really write a book in 9 days?"

Yes! Well 14 days, but 5 of those days I either did not write or I was coaching clients on how to retire, so I could not write. This always leads to the follow-up question: "How?!"

We know the average person can set a goal of 1000 words a day and in 30 days they will have 30k words. If they keep that up for two months, they will have 60k words. When writing a bestseller, your goal should be roughly 60,000-65,000 words. Yet that does not answer how I did it.... So how did I accomplish the task of becoming a bestseller in 9 days?

1. Know your strengths and weaknesses. Take me for example, I can't spell, have no idea about any form of grammar, tense, or many other things that my assistant picks on me for all the time. In fact, everyone I send text messages to, routinely laughs at how bad and utterly incoherent they are. Yet still, nine days later, there was over 69,000 words in my rough draft. So what was the solution? The same things I teach my coaching clients: outsource. When I take on new clients and they all want to have me retire them in a year, (6 months is the average), I make sure they double down on their strengths in their professional life and double down on their weaknesses in their personal life. This means if you suck at something, find someone else who doesn't. In other words, I wrote 5-20k words a day and went to bed. Magically, the next morning it was edited with notes for me to review. But how? My assistant Christine, who should win a price for patience and kindness. She would edit the document while I was sleeping, and since she

lives in the Philippines, we are 12 hours apart. And she would just knock it out at $4/hr.

2. Know you are going to throw A LOT out. My book was over 69k words, almost 70k words. However, we threw out probably another 5-15k words. They were simply not good. And I knew that.

3. Lastly, be honest with yourself. Let's say your favorite book is, on a scale from 1-10, it is a 10. Yours is going to be a 6...maybe a 7. Make peace with that. Your book is not designed to change the world in one print. It will take a few revisions and keep the purpose of your book top of mind, the entire time. The point is to get it out of your head, and then self-edit; over and over and over.

Bonus tip: Buy a lot of paper. You are going to print out your book over and over again. This will allow you to make changes faster and with more efficiency. Entire chapters will be moved, it is ok. That is the editing part, and the next stop on our Path to Publish.

Create your version of P.A.S.T.O.R.

- Go to becomingabestseller.com and either create a free account or log in to your existing Path to Publish
- Time to list:
    - P _____
    - A _____
    - S _____
    - T _____
    - O _____
    - R _____
    - What are your strengths?
    - What are your weaknesses?
- If you think your P.A.S.T.O.R. is not that organized or strong enough for your book, reach out to us at coaching@becomingabestseller.com and we'll help you with it.

EDITING:
MAKING IT
FINAL

Y ou've made it! Take a deep breath and save a copy somewhere. Either email it to yourself, or dump it off to either a USB drive or cloud storage. If you want to truly make your document safe, email it to a friend that you trust, with the instructions not to touch it. Why all the precaution? Because we are about to enter the editing phase. Before we start this phase, it is important to know this phase is the longest and the most tiresome. In most cases, this phase is indefinite as all pieces of work are truly never finished. This is again where our mantra of perfection is the enemy of execution.

EDITING TYPES

The type of editing can be dived into two distinctive categories; Developmental and Proofreading.

DEVELOPMENTAL EDITING

This is where you look at your book as a complete work and as a whole. Paragraphs, sentences, chapters can be moved around, changed, and possibly removed. It allows you to begin seeing your entire body of work in one overview. Imagine you are getting dressed to go out. This is the outfit that you are going wear, where you are going to go, and what movie you are going to see. Everything is fluid and in a state of flux. In this part of editing, the entire book can radically change. Therefore, this is the most expensive type of editing and can cost up to 7 cents a word and normally takes two rounds.

The second is called Proofreading and is the part that reminds us all of those horrid English tests we would take as children. Especially for me as I was someone who experienced failing English classes throughout my entire life. This is where we take on spelling, punctuation, grammar, tense, and so forth. Again, think about going out, this is where we shave our legs, pluck our eyebrows, brush our teeth, and make sure we have done our hair. It is detail time. It is some of the hardest to edit but luckily is only cost around .02 a word.

 ## WHO EDITS WHAT?

As with most up-and-coming bestselling authors, budget is always a tad bit tight. This is where a little bit of elbow grease and effort comes into play, in the format of Self-Editing.

The benefit of completing self-editing, at least for the first round, is two-fold. Firstly, it saves you money, secondly it must be done by you as it is your voice. For some of our authors who do a good enough job, it might be enough on its own. This comes down to experience, writing skills, and your standards. There are a few things you can do to make this a lot easier:

1. Read your book out loud — Do this line by line, word by word. You will most likely catch your errors as you read. Now that you have read it out loud, do it again, and again. It is the best way to catch your mistakes. As you read it out loud, take notes on the Developmental Editing changes you discover. The more you are exposed to your writing, the more changes that will occur.

2. Keep a note pad close — During this process, take notes of new things you want to add. Try not to stop, just take notes and push through.

3. By the third time, you should have reached the cleanest possible results, and it is time to ship it off to the editor or, if you are happy with it, go to publish. Always keep in mind that perfection is the enemy of execution.

4. Key note: Remember, you do not have to do this. None of the steps we recommend are required. However, self-editing will create a better book and help you reduce the costs of editing.

FINDING THE FLAWLESS EDITOR

Many authors get hooked on the idea of discovering the "right" or "perfect" editor that will magically transform their book into a New York Times Bestseller. They do exist. One of them is named Tahl Raz, and he charges mid-six figures and has a multiyear waiting list. For the rest of us normal people, we need something a lot more realistic.

Editors come in different shapes, sizes and talents. Deciding which one you would like is step one. Are you looking for someone to add content? Is this person just going to proofread? What about completing developmental editing? It is important the person understands your genre. If they have years of experience in nonfiction versus fiction, the tone of the edits will change. Once you decide on all of these things, we get to begin our search. In order to save on budget, you can always look within your trusted circle; Personal friend, family, or acquaintance. There are benefits and drawbacks to this and we do not recommend friends or family. Sure, they will be cheaper, however expense shows they are either far too nice or will change your message in its entirety. When it comes to an acquaintance, it is better as they are still vested in your success. The ideal is to simply outsource.

When outsourcing there are three places to look; Fiverr, Upwork, and a done-for-you solution.

Personally, we do not recommend Fiverr, as the quality of results are abysmal. Upwork on the other had has huge benefits. All of the members are tracked by reviews, exams, and experience. When you create and post your ad you can choose people based on location, hourly rate, and reviews. These are parameters that have proven to produce the most reliable results.

All applicants must have:

1. 90% approval rating
2. Have earned over $10,000
3. Based in the Philippines
4. Active within the last 2 weeks.

Once you have your candidate, check their portfolio, see the reviews and send them a small sample of your work. Ask yourself if they have done this type of work in the past. Remember some editors are non-fiction editors, while others are fiction. Some focus on fitness, and others one mental health. Pick one that aligns with you. Then review what they send back, if it is up to par. Plan an interview with them and get a feel for them. It is important that you like them and you connect with them. It is also important to make sure that they are responsive. Communication is key as they are going to be ripping your book apart and giving you raw feedback. Remember IT IS YOUR BOOK! They might not like things, they might want to change things, however it is your book. Don't forget to check the books they have edited before and how they have done professionally. Did they do well in the market you are trying to advance in?

Try and get a few pages, or even purchase one of the books they have edited in the past, so you can see their writing style. Typically, most will do a chapter, or at the very least a few pages. Chances are, if you like the few pages that they have completed in the past, you will probably like what they do for you.

If they don't pass the test, it will not be an issue, you will get a lot of applicants. A professional, seasoned editor with connections in the publishing industry can cost 8k and beyond. A professional from Upwork will cost you $800-$1500. Someone decent will be around $500. This is not a step you want to skip or go lazy on. It is important to spend the time. Try to keep in mind you will run into issues, it will not be perfect and you will most likely have multiple versions of your book as you find more mistakes, changes, and input. That is expected. We need to get the book to market.

You can always find other resources, but in this case, you get what you pay for.

NEGOTIATION

SAVING MONEY

So, you have found your consultant, and you are impressed by their work. Everything from their past work, to the communication, is amazing and you are ready to go. Except there is one last hurdle: price. You now must master negotiation. I get to cheat a little here because I am certified by Harvard on what they actually call Negotiation Mastery.

Let's start with a few things you need to know about any negotiation:

Basics of negotiation

Who has the power in the negotiation?
The person willing to walk away.

"BATNA" is an acronym which stands for 'Best Alternative to a Negotiated Agreement'[13]. BATNA answers the question: 'What would you do if you were not able to agree to a deal with your negotiation partner?'

What else, other than a deal, are you looking for? But that is not all. It is also crucial to assess the BATNA of the other side. The weakness of your own BATNA might not matter that much if the other side has no good alternative to doing business with you. If you are on a tight budget, you can offer the editor a portion of the sales. Or you can also offer to recognize them as you know your book is going to be a bestseller! It is a huge bonus for them on their resume. AND everyone loves to have their name in print. Also, offer them a place inside where you can put their name and a link to their website or portfolio so they can get more business.

"Reservation Value" is the least favorable point at which one will accept a negotiated agreement. For example, for a seller, this means the minimum amount they would be prepared to accept, while for a buyer it would mean the maximum that they would be prepared to pay. Unlike BATNA, the Reservation Value is always expressed as a number. It can be the same number that you can get without the negotiation, but it can also mean a different number. For example, imagine you are selling your car. Your relative tells you that he would buy it from you for $10,000 if you are not able to sell it elsewhere. But if you were okay to sell it for $10,000 to your relative, you might want other buyers to pay at least $11,000. In this case, the BATNA is selling to the relative for $10,000, but the Reservation Value is $11,000. While preparing for a negotiation, it is important to estimate the Reservation Value of your counterpart.

"Zone of Possible Agreement (ZOPA)"[14] is the range in which an agreement is satisfactory to both parties involved in the negotiation process. It is the range between each parties Reservation Values and is the overlap area that each party is willing to pay in a negotiation.

"Never be so sure of what you want that you wouldn't take something better."[15]

— Chris Voss

This is what is taught in every business school on the planet, and where it is not horrible, it is ineffective.

Recall our conversations about sales and how the human mind works. We, as creatures, will run from pain far faster than we will run towards pleasure. Back in 1979, Daniel Kahneman and Amos Tversky introduced us to the "loss aversion" principle. In its purest form, try to imagine this scenario: a friend offers to flip a coin and give you $5 if it lands on heads. However, if it lands on tails, you give her $5. Would you take that gamble? Probably not. Most of us would need far better odds. Instead of $5 to $5, we would need $10 to $5. In other words, the amount you could win would need to be at least twice as large as the amount you could lose. This is why we must truly listen and understand the person we are negotiating with. Just as in sales, we must be able to answer:

1. What do they want?
2. What pain are they in?
3. How can we help them thrive?
4. What human need are they constantly trying to fulfill?

For example, we are looking for a person to help us edit this book as my writing abilities are embarrassing. I put out an ad and we have a great deal of interest. One application was amazing, with over 100% reviews and 25% under budget. I reached out to her and during her conversation, it became clear she was not about the money, it was about the stability of the work. She wanted to know that she had guaranteed income for the weeks to come. I quickly told her we are editing multiple versions of the book and asked if she would be interested in becoming our go-to editor, even though we were not sure we could afford her. All she heard was 'guaranteed work', and magically another 10% dropped of the price without even asking.

We are taught that it is always about the money, yet it rarely is. It is about the illusion of control, comfort, time, respect, and rapport. The other side wants to feel they were treated fairly and with respect. There are so many factors in negotiation, far more than a simple section in this book could possible cover. For now, here are some key things to always remember:

1. It is about building rapport
2. Give them the illusion of control, let them say no. The faster you get them to a no, the faster you are to a yes.
3. Uncover what they really want, what drives them, and what pain they are in.
4. Once discovered, build helping you as the easiest way to solve those issues
5. Know exactly what you want, what your stretch goals are, and where you can give in.
6. Remember they need you, not the other way around. Always be ready to walk away.

THE LEADER WITHIN

You have found your team and written you book. Congratulations! Now the real work can begin. Any project manager, CEO, or single mom can tell you; managing is just advanced babysitting. You now have a team that is spread across the world. They need deadlines, accountability, and most of all a leader. More importantly, your bestseller needs you.

As you and your team work on elevating your connection to the point of being seamless, it is time to hold them accountable. The connection has allowed you to thrive through a few rounds with them and you have the ability to work together as a team. Now it is time to build your masterpiece. The goal is balance, accountability and deadline. It is critical to remember:

"What gets measured, gets done."

DEADLINES

We must have measured and strict deadlines.

When you hand over tasks for anything from edit, to cover design, to marketing, also ask yourself:

- What do I want?
- What am I willing to pay?
- When will I see a rough draft?
- When is the deadline; i.e. when MUST it be done?

A way to accomplish this is through something called milestones. The milestones should represent a clear sequence of events that incrementally build up until your project is complete. If you are making a logo, set time for when the first few drafts will be delivered, then when the edit of the first draft is ready and so you can move to the next step until completion. Without milestones throughout your project, it will simply not get completed. Remember to build in time for you as well; just because you see an edit does not mean you turn around that moment and send it back. We still need to make time to review and accept the changes as well. That takes time and must be put into the process and timeline.

With most edits, be prepared for three to five rounds. That includes both proofreading and developmental edits.

Pro Tip: Make sure you are both working on the same document at the same time. When changes are made to one and you are using a different version, time is lost, as is all the hard work. One of the best options for this is OneDrive. You can be live in a document at the same time your editor is in it as well. Best of all, OneDrive is free.

 ## COMMUNICATION IS KEY

As in all relationships, communication is key.

When it comes to communication, it is broken into two parts: systems and substance

i. Systems. Keep it simple

    a. USE SKYPE. It is easy, free and reliable.

    b. Use a dedicated time or scheduling app. There are dozens of free ones, but a simple reminder on your phone is best. If your editor is in the same time zone, great. If not, the two of you decide which one you will work out of and then go from there. Most vendors will adjust to your time zone to keep things easier.

    c. When you schedule time with any vendor, make sure they adhere to the appointments, as should you. Do not be late, do not treat them and their work with disrespect. It will dramatically change the output of the work.

ii. Substance

    a. OK, let's get this out of the way right now. Ready? Some of what you are going to write will be horrific. It will absolutely suck. It will be an embarrassment to the paper it is printed on. You can hate me for saying it, but it is critical that you get over this so when your editor says this, you know he/she is on your team. They are trying to help you, and your ego is not as important as your book. Breath through this, and get over it so you can move on.

    b. You and your editor must be able to be brutally honest with each other. It is critical! No holding back. If you like something, say it, if not, SAY IT and demand the same from them.

> Statements Like:
> Hey man I don't agree with that.
> I don't see it that way.
> Wow, this does not seem to work!
> Let's talk about this.

    c. Always try and have the conversation. Always try and connect.

When you hand in the book to your editor, YOU ARE NOT DONE! In fact, this might be the most frustrating and time-consuming part. If you want to just hand something over and move on with your life, hire a ghost writer. If not, be prepared to be open and put in the work to get your masterpiece where you want it. Remember they will only work as hard as you do. There will be remarks, suggestions, ideas, and markups. IT IS YOUR BOOK. Accept what you want to and reject whatever you don't, but you must go line by line with them. You are the final decision maker.

NEXT STEPS

Focus on finding the right editor for you.

- Go to becomingabestseller.com and either create a free account or log in to your existing Path to Publish
- Examine all the applicants and make sure that your editor is the perfect fit for your book's topic and genre.
- Have systems in place to make sure that deadlines are met.
- If your freelancer lives in a different time zone, choose a specific time that both of you could talk. Communication is key.
- If you are having problems setting your budget, or need help in choosing the right editor for you, reach out to us at coaching@becomingabestseller.com.

NOTES

PUBLISH

THE

DESIGN:

JUDGING

A BOOK

BY ITS

COVER

The book's design is one of the things that readers are attracted to, and for some, it could be the sole purpose of why exactly they bought your book (or not). When you pass by bookstores, you will see layer after layer of beautifully designed books, angled at specific degrees, with pin lights shining on them. Bookstores do that purposefully. They are showcasing these beautifully covered books to passers-by, with the hopes of attracting them into coming in to the store and purchasing one.

In fact, I have seen some books online that have really bad reviews, with readers saying things like, "The content is garbage, but the cover and layout are magnificent." The magnificent design was probably the reason why the reader bought the book, not thinking that the content was useless. This happens all the time, to be honest—we judge books by their covers. Another recent book that I've seen had white, blank pages in between texts, and some of the printed words were not legible, as if there had been a shortage of ink during the printing process. It's a sad reality but it does happen; this is why authors should never settle for mediocre overall designs.

When it comes to designing a book, there are basically five parts to it: the front cover, the front matter, the content, the back matter, and the back cover. Let's go over these five parts one by one, so that you can be guided accordingly. We will discuss what is included in each part, and its requirements.

FRONT COVER:

The front cover is the part of the book that the readers see first when the book is presented to them. Whether people are attracted to it will depend on your design per se. Some designs can be a bit cheesy, others are clever, while others simply have no impact at all. Also, you cannot please everyone, so what looks amazing to you, others might see as full of crap. However, this is not an excuse for you to create weak and mediocre designs. If you don't know how to design a book cover, there are websites and videos that teach you how to do it, but if you really have no knack for designing things, then you can just hire someone to do the designs for you. Just make sure that you guide them through the process, and since you have the best idea on what your book is all about, you can guide the designer on the look and feel of your cover. Another option is to look for existing designs and draw inspiration from them. If you are writing a romance novel, try to look for books in the same genre and combine ideas so that you can create your own. You can also post on forums, or even ask your friends—kind of crowdsourcing ideas for your cover.

FRONT MATTER:

The next part of the book is the front matter. Keep in mind that the front matter is different from the front cover, let's get that straight. A front cover is the glossy or matte covering of the book's front, where you can see the author's name, title, and a graphic representation of the book. On the other hand, the front matter is the first few pages that you see when you open the book cover. Remember when you were young and you had books at home with pages that only had the title written on it? Then you turn the next page, and you see another almost blank page with the same title written on it, but this time, the name of the author is included. Such redundancy was weird. Or so you thought. Turns out, those pages were needed in the publishing world.

There is no standard front matter for all books. Each book, depending on the genre and type of publication, will have different front matter contents. So let's go over some of the most common front matter parts:

a. **Half title:** The half title is a page in the book that only has the title written on it, nothing more.

b. **Title page(s):** The title page is similar to the half page; however, this time, the name of the author is included. This also depends on the type of book; however, it may also include:

    i.   Publisher's information
    ii.   Copyright information
    iii. ISBN
    iv. Edition
    v.   Publication date
    vi. Disclaimers
    vii. Warranties
    viii. Safety notes

c. **Dedication:** The dedication is the part that is written by the author, which includes the names of the people for whom the book was written.

d. **Table of Contents:** This is typically in the middle of the front matter. It may include a simple listing of the contents of the book, or it could also be very detailed with chapter descriptions.

e. **Acknowledgements:** This part is also written by the author and usually includes a little thank you to those who have helped in the book's publication.

f. **Foreword:** The foreword is a short piece of note, written by someone else other than the book's author. Usually, it explains the connection between the foreword writer and the author, or the story of the book itself.

CONTENT:

So, this is the entire interior of your book. This is the substance of your manuscript—the pages that will actually be read by most of your readers (let's admit it, we often skip the front matter part). During the writing phase, most of you have probably used Microsoft Word, WordPad, or other similar document writing programs. At this stage, your book is written in the standard 8.5" × 11" page size, with one-inch margins on the side. This is the standard in document writing, yes, but definitely not the standard for book writing. Depending on your book's genre, the size of your book will matter. Children's books usually are much larger than ordinary adult novels. I have seen self-help books that are also much larger than the standard novel size, so it really depends on your liking. There are no standard sizes, but the most common size is 6" × 9".

With your entire content being squished into a 6" × 9" page, it wouldn't make sense if you retain the one-inch margins on all sides. This is why there are guidelines when it comes to page sizes and margins, akin to the number of pages of your entire book. Below are the guidelines for the book margins:

Page count	Inside (gutter) margins	Outside margins (no bleed)	Outside margins (with bleed)
24 to 150 pages	0.375" (9.6 mm)	at least 0.25" (6.4 mm)	at least 0.375" (9.4 mm)
151 to 300 pages	0.5" (12.7 mm)	at least 0.25" (6.4 mm)	at least 0.375" (9.4 mm)
301 to 500 pages	0.625" (15.9 mm)	at least 0.25" (6.4 mm)	at least 0.375" (9.4 mm)
501 to 700 pages	0.75" (19.1 mm)	at least 0.25" (6.4 mm)	at least 0.375" (9.4 mm)
701 to 828 pages	0.875" (22.3 mm)	at least 0.25" (6.4 mm)	at least 0.375" (9.4 mm)

As you can see, depending on the number of pages, your inside margins and outside margins will vary. The inside margin is what we call the side that is bound by the spine, and the outside margin is what we call the side that is on the outer edge of the book.

If you have photos in your book, it is important that you consider the *bleed* in paperback versions. Bleed is a technical term used by publishers to describe the extra allowance that you put after the margin. It's just a few millimeters off the usual outside margins, but it is important in paperback publishing. Have you ever seen magazines that were cleverly printed so that the two sides look like one whole picture? Here is a good example of that:

Full Bleed   Final Trimmed Document

0.125"

Partial Bleed   Final Trimmed Document

If the bleed was not considered in this page, then there could be white spaces near the border. In the world of publishing, it is better to have photos that go over the edge as they will be trimmed eventually, than photos that fall short. The bleed is important to those who print full-page photos, so as not to mangle the photos during publishing. When publishers trim their books to the desired size, the extra allowance created by the bleeds will allow them to cut off the edges without distorting the photo when the book is bound.

BACK MATTER:

The back matter is almost similar to the front matter, except that it's located at the very end of your book, and it usually contains references to your content per se. After you type "the end" on your book, it doesn't mean that you're done, and you print it off, ready to be bound by the publishing house.

You still need to create the back matter, and what is found in your book's back matter will again depend on the type of publication and genre of your book. Let's take a look at some of the most common back matters in books:

a. **Bibliography:** This is often called the reference list. If you are writing a thriller novel, then there is no need for you to create one. However, for self-help books, scientific and historical publications, the bibliography is a must. It's impossible not to have one if you are basing things off reality. Readers would assume that all the things you have written in your book were originally yours. It's just impossible. Nothing is original now. Ideas bounce off from one mind to another, and after a few minutes of brainstorming, a new idea is born, but this new idea must have come from someone else's idea. So always cite your sources.

b. **Glossary:** The glossary is the part that explains the new terms, or colloquial slang you have used in the book. So, say you have used the term "yolo" in your book. Not everyone knows what this means (especially the older generation). To reduce confusion, a glossary must be created, explaining what "yolo" meant. The glossary is usually alphabetized, and includes specialized terms and uncommon ones.

c. **Index:** The index is the part people use to find specific terms in the book. This part is also alphabetized, just like the glossary. However, the difference is that, in the index page, it doesn't matter if the words you included are specialized terms or ones with colloquial meaning—as long as it is important in the book, you put it in the index. To give you an example, say you have a character in your book named Grace, and she has been mentioned 11 times. All those pages where she has been mentioned, you have to list in the index, so that if readers go, "Oh, I forgot what Grace shared in the group during the session," the reader can then go back to these pages with ease.

BACK COVER:

In paperbacks, this part is to be designed as well by a professional designer. The design should match what you have on the front, except in some cases wherein you want to shock people with the message that you have written on the back part. This part is your chance to communicate with your readers, and so it should be aesthetically pleasing.

The back cover includes the book description, the author bio, optional testimonials, your photo, publishing company's logo, barcode, and ISBN. If you do not style this part well, your back cover will be hard to read, and so readers might just skip your book and pick another. This is something that you don't want to happen. I have seen a book with a black back cover and scarlet red text on it, and it was a pain to read.

WHERE TO GET IT DESIGNED

Now that the book parts have been discussed briefly, your next decision is whether you will design it yourself, or have it done by a professional. If you don't have the knack for design, then the best solution is to hand it off to someone else who knows what they're doing.

There are various ways that you can deal with your design issue: either hire a freelancer, or hire a design company. There is nothing wrong with hiring either of the two, just make sure that you communicate well with them, and that you have an open communication with your assigned designer so that you two can tell each other if the design is a flop or not.

First, we have Fiverr. Fiverr is a freelancing platform where the freelancers offer "gigs" or services for as low as $5. What? $5?! Yes, some, but not all. Usually, they offer a $5 gig, but due to the add-ons that you have added in your cart, you will still end up paying $30 — $50 on average. It also depends on the job. If you have a custom job for your book design, it will definitely cost more, and one gig might even reach $150 — $200. However, some of them accept gigs for less than $80. Yes, you are going to save a lot of money, yet the product is normally a reflection of that. Fiverr has some diamonds in the rough, but they are hard to find. To be honest, 99% of the time, I don't recommend it. It normally looks like you spent $5.

The second option is Upwork. This platform is full of free-lancers with great potential. This will put you back about $500-$1000 for a really amazing design. Mine was $70, but I was involved a lot, and I purchased the artwork in advance to supply it to the designer. If you want to look for artwork inspirations, use Bing and search for what you are looking for. If you are lucky, you can zero in on one design and go from there. However, once you do have one, use Upwork.com to hire a designer, and talk to them for the modifications that you need.

The third, and most expensive option, is to hire a design company. Design companies are great and you can expect quality output from them. However, they can be quite expensive, and might bleed you dry if you don't have enough budget for the design alone. But if you have the means to hire them, then do so, as design companies produce the best results among the three that we have mentioned. Their designs are professionally done, and they have a pool of people in their team, brainstorming about what's best for your book. Their designs usually convert to more sales since their creations are usually well though-out and are based on research (what design would work best in your niche). Since design companies don't usually need your involvement in the design process, this will allow you to focus on content creation and forget about the designing stage. Should they need your approval, that is the only time that you need to get involved, but apart from that, you can just leave the project with them, and allocate your energy to marketing, for example.

THE DESIGNER

So, before you create an account with the sites that we gave, let's backtrack a little bit and make sure that you have a few designs in mind before hiring a designer. You can't just hire someone and tell them that you wrote a book on sailing and ask them to design what they think is good. You have to give them a concept, at least, to start with. You could write a book, so I assume you can be creative enough to come up with a one-page design concept. Even if the concept is still raw, it doesn't matter, as long as you have something to give to your designer. Remember, they are designers, not psychics. They don't know what looks good for you, and what looks weird, so you have to make sure that you have a concept for them to work with.

Imagine this scenario: You hire a designer and tell him that your book is about sailing, and that he needs to create a design based on sailing. The designer then creates a mock up consisting of a yacht with people on it, because this is how he understood what sailing meant. You reject it since your book is actually about the sport of sailing. The designer then creates another one with a sailing boat in the middle of still waters. However, this is not how you wanted to portray sailing as a sport, since you wanted an exciting cover. You see what's wrong here? If you gave the designer even a few hints on what you wanted to see on the cover, then he could have gotten the concept on the first try.

So, the best way to deal with your design problem is to first look for concepts, browse pictures that you like, and even the fonts that you would like the designer to use. Make sure that the photos that you choose are connected with your book and inspire you.

NEGOTIATION

After a few days of brainstorming, by now you should already have a concept in mind (and the photos saved in your computer), ready to be given to your prospective designer. Now, we get on with the hiring process. If you opted for a freelance designer, that's ok, too. I am here to guide you through the hiring process, and I will give you tips as to how you can negotiate the prices.

It doesn't matter what freelancing platform you use; they all are similar in terms of the hiring process. Once you have posted your job for a book designer, an influx of applicants will submit their applications and you now have to sift through them and weed out the bad apples. As an employer, you will then be allowed to view their profiles and the reviews their previous clients have left them. Ask yourself, did they work on a similar project in the past? Look at their portfolios. Designers usually have portfolios attached to their profiles, and sometimes, they even have a website displaying all the works they have done in the past. Did you like their work? If you did, you can shortlist them so that you can go back to them at a later time.

After shortlisting five to ten applicants, try to rank them from highest to lowest. Get the highest five and start a conversation with them. You have to be very patient when dealing with them, and you also have to ensure that you have meticulously described your vision. Try to assess who is the best designer for you, based on your conversation with them. Remember that these freelancing platforms are open to anyone, which means you will get applicants from all over the world. Take note of how well you and the designer communicate with each other. Does he understand your concept well? If the designer's first language is not English, that might be a problem in the future when you are giving revisions and so on. So make sure that you are comfortable with the designer that you choose.

When it's time to hire someone, go back to what I have shared about negotiation. It is your book, your money, so you have the power to walk away. If the designer asked for $500 for the entire book (from cover to cover), that's already a good price, however you can always negotiate for better deals. These are the different ways on how you can negotiate with your designer:

a. **Name placement:** Tell them that in exchange for a better deal, they can always put their name in the artwork and sign it. Some designers like this idea, especially those who are still getting their names out there.

b. **Website link:** Apart from name placement, another way is to offer them a space on your back cover for their website link. This idea will benefit both of you, and who wouldn't want this? It's free marketing for them basically. They just need to design one book, and every time the book is sold, one person will be able to see their website link, and that's a potential customer for them.

c. **Recognition:** You can also offer to mention their name in your marketing paraphernalia. You can put their name on your press releases, so this is another avenue of free marketing for their design business. If you are planning to submit press releases to big media companies like Yahoo!, CNN, Fox, Forbes, or Inc, this will surely benefit them a lot.

d. **Book Sales:** I cannot really recommend this last part, but it worked in the past. Tell them that, in exchange for a lower price on the design, you can give them a certain percentage for every book sale. Some designers see the bigger picture, and might agree to giving you a huge discount for their service in exchange for, say, 3% of commission for every book that you sell. Again, this is not something that I would recommend since every percent of sales you give away hits your bottom line.

COMMUNICATION

Now, what if your designer has given you the first draft and you didn't like it? How would you communicate the revisions that you want done on your design? Sure, you can type and describe everything in narrative form, however, we are living in the 21st century, and we have a ton of ways to show people visually how we want things done.

A great tool that I use with my assistant is Loom (https://www.loom.com). This program is free to download and use. But what can you do with Loom? After downloading the program, you need to open the first draft that your designer submitted to you. Tell him the things you liked and things you didn't like by pointing it out with your cursor and talking on your microphone. This is by far the most effective way of giving out instructions as people now are very visual. There will be fewer errors since you are showing them exactly what to replace and modify, as if you are right beside them. Just like when you're in the office, and your co-worker calls for help. They will point with their mouse the things that are unclear to them, and you discuss it with them. Since you and your designer are probably living countries apart, Loom is the best option that you have.

If round one wasn't to your liking, you can always ask your designer for concepts. Be open to the ideas of others. They probably have done similar projects in the past, so gaining an insight or two from their experience won't hurt you. They are by far more experienced than you in the design department (that is why you opted to have your design outsourced in the first place, right?), so whenever they give you ideas, don't shut them down.

If you have a marketing team in place, you also need some input from them regarding your design. They have done tons of research on your book already, and have been in the trade for years, so they know exactly what will work and what won't work.

In toto, in terms of getting other people's perspectives, you only have to listen to two other groups apart from yourself: your designer and your marketing team.

OTHERS' INPUT

Now, we are going to discuss the final design input. Once you and your designer have agreed that the design he submitted is the final one, you have to show it to other people to get their feedback. Much like naming a child, some will hate it, some will love it, and everyone will give you their two cents. That's ok though, as you need as much feedback as you can gather at this point. Post it on your social media, and if you have a lot of design, perhaps you commissioned your designer to design more than two designs, then create a poll on social media and ask them which design they prefer.

You must accept the fact that the first round of design/s will not be amazing. Nobody ever gets it on the first try. This is now your chance to get feedback from your friends. Encourage people to tell you if they liked your design or not, and ask them to make suggestions as well. Let the changes come and go. Weigh their suggestions and see which ones make sense.

Remember, don't settle. The saying, "don't judge a book by its cover" is popular, but sadly, untrue. We do judge books by their covers, and people will also judge you based on the cover that you create. If your cover looked like it was made by someone who just learned photoshop, it will show, and people like nice and shiny things, so they probably won't like your cover if it looks basic. Whereas, if it looks intriguing and beautifully crafted, your book will be lifted on the shelves a hundred times more. Remember, once you make it big, you will be taking pictures with your book for years to come, so make sure it will be something you adore.

Time to get on with your book's design.

- Go to becomingabestseller.com and either create a free account or log in to your existing Path to Publish
- Time to outline the parts of your book. Have you hired your designer for the following?
  - Front Cover
  - Content
    - Margins
    - Alignment
    - Bleed
  - Back Cover
- Ask others how they feel about your overall book design.
- List and weigh on both the positive and negative things that people have said about your design/layout.
- Create a Loom account to effectively communicate with your designer.
- If you need help with your book's paperback layout and need additional opinions about your designs, reach out to us at coaching@becomingabestseller.com and we will help you with it.

THE

PUBLISHING:

FORMATS,

DESIGNS,

AND

DESCRIPTIONS

THAT INCREASE

SALES

t's now time to discuss, in detail, the publishing requirements of your book. Since you will be doing two formats,
the ebook version and the paperback, you need to know
their differences when it comes to formatting. Both
formats are not the same, mainly because ebooks are digital,
and will be read using tablet, iPad, or Kindle; whereas for paperbacks, the publishing company will print it out, and there
are a lot of things to consider. We have discussed in detail all
the requirements for the paperback; now it's time to discuss
the ebook requirements.

Forget about what you have learned about paperback formatting, as the ebook format is a bit more lenient when it
comes to overall formatting. Let's start with line spacing and
indentations. Microsoft Word is the most popular document
writing program as it is available for both Mac and Windows,
so these guidelines will be for the said program. Kindle
doesn't recognize tab spacing, so you have to ensure that
you have set up indentation to 0.2". Some books don't indent,
and that's ok too. If you don't use indent, you don't need to
do this step. The line spacing should always be set to 0 pt. as
you don't need that extra space after each line.

The start of every chapter should have chapter titles (and I
don't mean custom titles, even "Chapter 1", "Chapter 2", etc.
will work). However, it needs to be started on a new page, and
should not be connected with the last paragraph of your last
chapter. In Microsoft Word, highlighting the words "Chapter
1", and changing the heading style to whatever you think is

best for your book's look, will make your chapter headings pop out and will also create a hyperlinked bookmark on your ebook. This is essential with ebooks since ebooks are interactive and you can place hyperlinks wherever you want.

When it comes to images, make sure that you have it centered when you insert the picture onto your book. Don't just copy and paste a picture from your source; make sure that you do it properly through the Insert feature of Microsoft Word. There are times that photos are not being copied over when you do the usual copy and paste, so do that extra step just to be sure.

You also have to take advantage of the ebook's hyperlinking feature, so you have to create an interactive table of contents. You can hyperlink each chapter, and set it up so that when the reader clicks on a chapter or page, the ebook will automatically scroll to that page. You can't do this on paperback, and this is one of ebook's wonders that many authors take advantage of.

As for the margins, we have mentioned that you need to forget all the margins and alignments that you have learned for paperback, as ebook versions are totally different. With the ebook version, every side should have the same margin size, and we generally recommend 0.5" all around. Remember, not all tablets and readers are the same. Some readers prefer big texts, especially those who are having difficulties reading small texts. With the established 0.5" on all sides, the readers can surely customize their reading experience without you having to worry about any text loss. When you go beyond the recommended 0.5", your book will look like a receipt, and you don't want for that to happen. That is just aesthetically unpleasant and worse, readers won't be able to read the contents of your book. Make sure, as well, that all your margins are positive numbers. It could be an honest mistake on your end that you put a little minus sign (-) before the number, and this will ruin your entire layout. Words will be cut off from the sides of your book.

When it comes to the page size, ebooks don't really have a set standard for the sizing. However, because of the different available ebook readers and tablets on the market, the only recommended size when creating your ebook is 8.5" × 11". Yes, that would be the standard page size in Microsoft Word when you first open a new document. So, hooray for the non-technical people out there, as there is nothing you need to do when it comes to adjusting the page size! Just make sure that it is in portrait layout, as opposed to landscape, but usually, when you open a new document, the default one is already in portrait. Remember there are readers that use iPads to read ebooks. If you format the page so that it fits the most common screen sizes such as 4" × 6", 5.5" × 8.5", or 5" × 7", then your ebook will look bad on larger iPad screens. So, to fit all screens, set the page size to the default 8.5" × 11".

AUDIOBOOK

Another format that we have not mentioned before is the audiobook. This is not a common format, as not all authors publish audiobooks, but if you want to reach more readers, then might as well publish an audiobook format. Apart from giving the blind community the chance to read your book, there are also other readers who prefer audiobooks since they multitask and they could listen to it while doing something else like driving or cooking.

It's not enough that you record your book using any recorder you can find. Sure, it will be convenient for you, but then the sound quality of your finished product will be questionable. After spending all that money on the layout of your ebook and paperback versions, you don't want to release a mediocre audiobook after all, right? Go all the way, and make sure that everything that you release with your name on it is spectacular.

SET UP:

So, how do you create an amazing audiobook version of your book? Simple. Set up a home studio. A spare room in your house won't be enough; you need to soundproof it. You don't want your readers to hear doors closing in between your audio recordings. Spend some money on making your room soundproof and you will benefit from it. You can later use the soundproofing materials in your room to ensure a good night's sleep if you are so worried about spending all that money. Next, you should have a comfortable chair. You will be reading for hours, so make sure that the chair you are using is as comfortable as it can get. Also, get a chair that won't squeak, as this will ruin your recording. Some audiobook readers have a very keen sense of hearing, so this will be distracting for them, not to mention irritating.

You also need to have a very good setup. Invest in a good condenser microphone that could filter out your breathing noises. Condenser microphones are excellent for studio re-cordings, and this is what podcast hosts are normally using. Windproof foams and feathers, as well as spit back screens, are available on the market for a very cheap price, so don't forget to purchase one for your microphone. Also purchase a microphone stand so that the volume of the sound doesn't change throughout your recording. If you've decided to hold the microphone while recording, you might hold it too close or too far from your mouth, which will both result in bad audio quality.

NARRATION:

Before you start recording, you have to practice first. Nobody gets it on the first try, and there will be times that you will need to redo some parts because of bad pronunciation or a slipup in the words. So, to eliminate these bad recordings, you need to practice reading, and repeat over and over again the words that you find challenging. Psychological is different from physiological, and if you have these two words in your book, then you might interchange both in the recording and this will not only ruin the audio output, but also confuse your readers, as both words have different meanings.

Also, make sure that you have two to three different colored pens when preparing for the recording. This is useful if you have conversations between two people in your book, and you need to know which character is talking. Some ebooks only maintain one voice and that's ok; you don't need to actually hire other people to do the other voices and create a radio drama-like audiobook. However, if you are doing one voice only, the emotions of the character in your book differ, so character A could be angry, and character B could be sad. If both characters talk, the colored highlights will help you determine the correct tone for each voice.

RECORDING BASICS:

Now, before you do the actual recording, you need to be wary about your food intake. What? What's the connection between my food and my recording?! Apparently, a lot. High protein food makes your stomach quiet. The last thing you want is your stomach grumbling when recording some lines. Avoid starches, as these make your stomach rumble. Eat a couple of green apples since this minimizes mouth noises, and totally avoid dairy products as these irritate the throat.[16] Also, before you enter your recording room, make sure that you put your phone on silent, and leave it outside. Do not bring it inside the room even if it is in silent mode, as it might interfere with the recording quality of your audio output. This might also distract you from speaking your lines as you might see a notification, and the moment you take your eyes off your book, then that would mean an unnecessary pause that you need to edit out.

In terms of using text-to-speech services, although they are very convenient, you should never use these programs as they do not sound natural. Even though technology has improved a lot in the last decade, we still haven't developed a machine or program that could convert text to speech like a normal human. They are normally monotonous, and you can tell that they are not human since the pace of how they read the text is not steady at all. Sometimes, they read so fast that the words almost overlap each other, sometimes, it's good. It actually depends on the way the words were recorded by humans during the program development. This can be quite distracting to your listeners, who are expecting good, steady pacing when listening to your audiobook.

Each upload must be free of sounds that aren't supposed to be included in the recording. This can be very distracting to the reader and may sound unprofessional. Sounds like mic pops and mouse clicks can take away a reader's interest in listening to your book further. This is why it is important to get all the required equipment before you start recording. Also, it may be helpful to actually have you read from your tablet or iPad to minimize any mouse clicks, page turns and other extra noises that can be picked up by your microphone. These noises can elicit bad reviews and this is the last thing that you want to have on your Amazon book page as this can hurt your book reputation and sales.

You should also record a separate sample file from your book, and it should not include any explicit material. This sample can be previewed by anyone, and it should start with your narration, not music fillers or opening credits. It should be a sample of what your readers will hear when they purchase your book. Some readers are very picky when it comes to choosing the audiobook that they will listen to next. They oftentimes will pick one by the tone of the voice, the gender, how loud the audio recording is, etc. Some of these you cannot control, and you cannot please every listener out there. They just have preferences. However, for the overall quality of your audiobook, this is definitely something you can manage, so make sure that you produce a superb sample and audiobook audio file. Amazon will not cut a part of your audio and display it as a sample. You have to manually submit one.

It is also important that you record a short 15 to 30 seconds of "roomtone", as this will be useful for editing later on. You can use this to cut and fill in pauses if you have missed a pause during recording. A short one to five seconds of roomtone is required for every section. This will be your readers' cue that they have reached the beginning or end of your book's section and it also helps with the successful encoding of your audiobook into many formats.

Now, for the technical specifications[17] of your file, you also need to "master edit" your audio so that it measures between -23dB and -18dB RMS, as this is the requirement for audio books. This ensures that your audio files are neither too loud, nor too soft for the listener's ears. It would be a pain if your readers had to keep adjusting the volume while listening to your audiobook. The maximum peak value of your audiobook should not be higher than -3dB to eliminate distortion. This can heavily reduce the quality of your reader's listening experience and may result in a negative review. Also, if there is a peak noise requirement, there is also a noise floor requirement, and it should not exceed -60dB RMS. Background noises such as static sounds, air blowing, or basically anything that can distract the listener, are not allowed in your audiobook recording. When you export your audio, make sure that the bit rate is 192kbps or higher 44.1kHz MP3, Constant Bit Rate (CBR) as this will produce a crisper sound. You don't want people to max up their volumes, and still struggle with what you're saying. You can definitely upload something higher like 256kbps or 320kbps, but the difference between 192kbps and higher bit rates is negligible.

When saving your audio files, don't splice your entire book into one big audio file. Although, when you purchase an audiobook, you do get only one file, however, when submitting your audio files, you need to split it by chapters. This way, readers can navigate through your files more easily. Each section should not be longer than 120 minutes.

We have given you some tips regarding the editing, however, if you are not a technical person and don't really know how to use audio editing software such as Audacity and the like, you might as well have it professionally done. You can go back to the guide we have detailed in the previous sections on how to hire a designer for your book, but this time, look for an audiobook creator or an audio editor. With audiobook creators, they usually know the requirements of audiobooks and you don't need to remind them about the guidelines. However, if you opt for just audio editors (as they might be cheaper), you need to communicate with them meticulously, and tell them what needs to be in an audiobook. This option is much easier for your part, and you can assure that your audiobook will be close to perfect since it was edited by a professional.

NEXT STEPS

Time to create your digital downloads.

- Go to becomingabestseller.com and either create a free account or log in to your existing Path to Publish
- Ebook checklist:
  - Margins
  - Alignments
  - Final check on ebook previewers such as Adobe Digital Editions or Kindle Previewer
- Audiobook checklist:
  - Prepare your diet (food intake)
  - Gather all the required audio paraphernalia
  - Correct decibels for the recording
  - Use roomtones in the beginning and end of every chapter
  - Hire an editor who can master audio files
- If you want suggestions and help with your ebook and audiobook, contact us at coaching@becomingabest-seller.com and we'll help you with it.

NOTES

BOOK DESCRIPTION: YOUR TICKET TO SELLING MORE

By now, you probably already have a working book title, and have commissioned a professional designer to do the front cover. However, you're still missing a few important things.

Sure, the front cover will make people grab your book from the shelf, but it's actually the back cover that makes them buy it. Why? It's because that's where your book description is written. This is the make or break factor when it comes to book sales. The content of your book may be great—heck, your ideas might even eradicate all kinds of cancers—but, how will people know that your book is good if you have a mediocre description? The book cover makes people pick up your book, yes, but the description makes them purchase it. Those are two different things, and as far as most authors are concerned, of course, book sales are more important.

WHY IT MATTERS

The book description is the part of the book that makes your readers want to purchase your book. Imagine a salesman selling cars. The salesman sees a young couple looking at a brand-new convertible, and of course, he swoops in like a vulture and grabs the opportunity. The fact that the couple are looking at it means they are already interested in what they see. This is similar to readers grabbing your book from the shelf. But of course, it's not just the looks of the car that they're interested in. Does the car fit their needs?

Maybe yes, since they are a childless couple. Is the trunk enough to fit in a three-day surfing vacation in Malibu? Probably not, since their huge surfboard won't fit in the trunk and there is no roof rack whatsoever. Book buyers also go through the same thing with the description. It's their only way to see what's inside the book, since most bookstores prohibit reading. They weigh the pros and cons of buying the book, and if they don't like what they've read, they put the book back on the shelf.

This is why the book description is very important. It acts as a pitch to your prospective customers, and frankly, it is your one chance to convince others why they need to buy your book. Not to pressure you further, but most descriptions are only 200 words long, so you have a slim window to do all the convincing that you need to do in order to sell.

THE ELEMENTS OF A GOOD BOOK DESCRIPTION

So how exactly do you write a good description? There are basically five elements that you need to consider when writing a description.

First is the **hook**. A hook, as self-explanatory as it can get, is the sentence that hooks you into reading more. It should be an attention-grabber, much like the headlines of a newspaper. When you pass by a newspaper shop and you see the headlines of one of the dailies, you stop and try to read the subheadings, right? The same goes for hooks. Their only purpose is to intrigue the reader so that they don't put the book down right away.

Remember, people today have short attention spans, so if you give them the reason to move on to the next book, even before they finish reading your 200-word description, are you actually expecting them to buy the book and finish the entirety of it? I don't think so. Generally, the first line of the description focuses on the most sensational fact of your book, or the boldest claim.

Second is **pain**. So hypothetically, you have created the best hook you could ever think of. Great! Now you have grabbed the attention of your prospective customer, and there is no turning back. The next step is to actually feel their pain and write a couple of sentences about it. What niche are you targeting? What do you think are their problems? What aspirations do they have? Do they have questions in life that can't be answered by any other book? Addressing the pain of someone is how you actually get their full attention. It means that you totally understand where they're coming from, and your book is your way of communicating with them.

Third is **pleasure**. At this point, you have already indicated their pain. Now is the time that you assure them that you can address it. If done right, the pleasure part lets them know that you have the answers to their problems. It creates an emotional connection with them by showing what they will feel after they finish reading your book.

If your book is about making millions with little investment, do you give them ideas of startup businesses with only $1,000 in capital? Is your book about losing weight? Are you giving them novel ideas on how to lose weight, which they have not tried before? Or maybe your book's about finding happiness in spite of feeling lost and empty inside? Perhaps you went through the same phase, and are willing to share what you did to get out of it. Make sure that you clearly indicate what they will get from the book. People love results, and once they see it, they will hold on to it.

Fourth is **legitimacy**. If you are a "nobody", of course people won't listen to you. No matter how fallacious it may be, we can't deny the fact that people listen to authority. Why do you think print and television commercials work? Are you familiar with one of the Kardashian siblings, Kylie Jenner? Why do you think her lipsticks sell like hot cakes even though they're overpriced? It's because people see how wonderful and plump her lips are, and how good they look on pictures and videos, that they actually see themselves looking like her when they use her lipstick. Maybelline even offers more shades than Kylie's, but her lipsticks usually sell out after a few days of coming back in stock. They actually forget for a minute that Kylie even admitted to using lip fillers[18], so their lips will never look exactly like hers, no matter what shade they use.

So how does this apply to your book description? Putting an actual line or phrase in your description that describes who you are and why people should listen to you is a great idea, as it will help with your book's legitimacy. If your book is about marriage counseling, then add a short line explaining that you are a practicing marriage counselor, and have helped × number of clients in your 15 years of practice.

However, just to be clear—you don't need to be a professional to claim legitimacy. Experiences also count. Back in 2010, there was a 17-year-old man named Steve Ortiz[19], who used the power of barter to acquire a Porsche convertible. What item did he start with? A used cellphone. He posted the used cellphone on Craigslist and bartered it for an iPod touch, then for a dirt bike, after that, for a MacBook Pro laptop, and not long after, he had a 1987 Toyota 4Runner in his hands. Then he bartered that car for a Ford Bronco SUV, and finally, a Porsche. If Steve writes a book in the future about Craigslist and how to utilize it to your advantage, and actually includes in his book description this story of cellphone to Porsche, would you buy the book? Hell yes!

The fifth and last element is open loop. So by now, you already have most of your book description written, and it's just missing one last detail. You already have described their pain, offered ways to solve it, but you also have to leave a small key piece out. This will leave them wanting more and make your book more enticing. Just like movie trailers, they actually only show the juiciest parts of the movie, but leave some of the fun parts out, or even pose a question at the very end to make you want more, and actually watch it in the theaters.

However, make sure that you are not making your readers struggle to understand what your book is about. This is true for most how-to or self-help books. People love to know the basics of "what" and "how", most especially if the idea is new.

EXAMPLES OF GREAT BOOK DESCRIPTIONS

4-Hour Work Week by Tim Ferriss[20]

Forget the old concept of retirement and the rest of the deferred-life plan–there is no need to wait and every reason not to, especially in unpredictable economic times.

Whether your dream is escaping the rat race, experiencing high-end world travel, earning a monthly five-figure income with zero management, or just living more and working less, The 4-Hour Workweek is the blueprint.

This step-by-step guide to luxury lifestyle design teaches:

- How Tim went from $40,000 per year and 80 hours per week to $40,000 per month and 4 hours per week
- How to outsource your life to overseas virtual assistants for $5 per hour and do whatever you want
- How blue-chip escape artists travel the world without quitting their jobs
- How to eliminate 50% of your work in 48 hours using the principles of a forgotten Italian economist
- How to trade a long-haul career for short work bursts and frequent "mini-retirements"

WHAT MAKES THIS A GOOD DESCRIPTION?

1. Tim's first sentence tells you right away why this book will matter to you. Why wait for real retirement at 60+? Why not retire now?

2. The bulleted form information actually helps with understanding what the book is about. Remember, people have short attention spans, so putting most of your text in bullet form actually makes the reader read them all.

3. The contrast between the broad goal on the first sentence, and the super-specific bulleted information, actually make the readers want to know more. They are now intrigued and would like to know how Tim teaches the "4-Hour Work Week".

Vivid Vision by Cameron Herold[21]

Many corporations have slick, flashy mission statements that ultimately do little to motivate employees and less to impress customers, investors, and partners.

But there is a way to share your excitement for the future of your company in a clear, compelling, and powerful way and entrepreneur and business growth expert, Cameron Herold, can show you how.

Vivid Vision is a revolutionary tool that will help owners, CEOs, and senior managers create inspirational, detailed, and actionable three-year mission statements for their companies. In this easy-to-follow guide, Herold walks organization leaders through the simple steps to creating their own Vivid Vision, from brainstorming to sharing the ideas, to using the document to drive progress in the years to come.

By focusing on mapping out how you see your company looking and feeling in every category of business, without getting bogged down by data and numbers, Vivid Vision creates a holistic road map to success that will get all of your teammates passionate about the big picture.

Your company is your dream, one that you want to share with your staff, clients, and stakeholders. Vivid Vision is the tool you need to make that dream a reality.

WHAT MAKES THIS A GOOD DESCRIPTION?

1. Cameron directly attacked corporations' mission statements, and a lot of people will agree with him that these statements do little in terms of motivating people, so people know it's a piece of crap. Since a lot of people can relate to it, people are now interested in reading more.

2. His book description actually uses what we call buzzwords, and though we don't really recommend using one, it depends on the nature of your book really. For business books, it's ok to use it, and since Cameron's book is business-natured, then it's actually good that he used some buzzwords like, "progress", "simple steps", and "easy to follow".

3. His book definition clearly illustrates that he knows what the reader is going through (pain) and the benefits they will get from reading his book (pleasure). To explain it further, he articulated the pain correctly, which is, "slick, flashy mission statements that ultimately do little", and offers a "detailed, actionable three-year mission statements for their companies" as a solution.

EXAMPLES OF BAD BOOK DESCRIPTIONS

The Hard Thing About Hard Things by Ben Horowitz[22]

Ben Horowitz, co-founder of Andreessen Horowitz and one of Silicon Valley's most respected and experienced entrepreneurs, offers essential advice on building and running a startup—practical wisdom for managing the toughest problems business school doesn't cover, based on his popular ben's blog.

While many people talk about how great it is to start a business, very few are honest about how difficult it is to run one. Ben Horowitz analyzes the problems that confront leaders every day, sharing the insights he's gained developing, managing, selling, buying, investing in, and supervising technology companies. A lifelong rap fanatic, he amplifies business lessons with lyrics from his favorite songs, telling it straight about everything from firing friends to poaching competitors, cultivating and sustaining a CEO mentality to knowing the right time to cash in.

Filled with his trademark humor and straight talk, The Hard Thing About Hard Things is invaluable for veteran entrepreneurs as well as those aspiring to their own new ventures, drawing from Horowitz's personal and often humbling experiences.

WHAT MAKES THIS A BAD DESCRIPTION?

Ben included in his book description a short blurb about his accomplishments, which is great since it helps with his legitimacy as an author of the subject. However, if I don't know who he is, or don't know anything about him, why would I even want to read more? His hook is missing and he certainly didn't grab my attention with the first sentence.

Coercion: Why We Listen to What "They" Say by Douglas Rushkoff[23]

Noted media pundit and author of Playing the Future, Douglas Rushkoff, gives a devastating critique of the influence techniques behind our culture of rampant consumerism. With a skilled analysis of how experts in the fields of marketing, advertising, retail atmospherics, and hand-selling attempt to take away our ability to make rational decisions, Rushkoff delivers a bracing account of media ecology today, consumerism in America, and why we buy what we buy, helping us recognize when we're being treated like consumers instead of human beings.

WHAT MAKES THIS A BAD DESCRIPTION?

Douglas' description is 84 words long, which is great, as short descriptions generally do better than long ones, however, 84 words is too short to really convey what your book is about. This is a perfect example of overselling the book, but not doing it right. His description does not even connect with the readers, since it is not compelling or engaging to begin with.

BOOK DESCRIPTION BEST PRACTICES

First, it is important to never think of book descriptions as synonymous with book synopses. Most new authors are thrilled with the idea of summarizing their work in a short blurb, and putting everything in the book description section. Please don't do that.

The book description is basically an advertisement; it's your one chance to tell the readers why they should buy your book. Just like movies, it is your trailer and it should convince the readers to take action and buy your book.

Second, you should use compelling keywords in your book description. Think of high traffic keywords that will make your book appear more often in search engine searches. The better your keywords are, the better its reach will be in the market. If a sports magazine decided to write a book, they would, of course, include names of A-listers in their book description, as people tend to search for their names. Apart from using high traffic keywords, using words that evoke certain emotions can also be effective for readers. They might be searching for words such as "bankruptcy", "divorce", and "depression", all of which evoke emotions, and if you have one of these in your book description, then your book will definitely show up in the search results.

Third, keep it short. Again, short descriptions are better than long ones. Remember, the attention span of an average person is short, so make sure that you write a short, but informative book description. All the information that the reader needs to know (plus, a little cliffhanger at the end) should be included, and it should be well within the 200-word range.

Fourth, keep the writing as simple as possible. Create simple sentences when writing your book description. The last thing that you want is a confused reader who can't comprehend what you want to convey.

Fifth, write the description in a third person voice. Never write it in your author voice, but write it as someone else.

Sixth, don't be insecure about other published books. Stop comparing your work with others. It is not right. Every author is unique, so comparing your book with other books will usually make you feel inferior. So if you feel like mentioning another book in your description, then make sure that you fashion it as a quotation, rather than as a comparison.

Lastly, try to let others write your book description for you. You have written 60,000 words for your book already. You know it inside out. I know a few authors who are struggling to write their own book descriptions mainly because they have the tendency to include a bunch of information in it. Ask a close friend of yours to read your book and write the description for you. Perhaps they have a better grasp on the major points that you have in your book? Also, they will be much more objective than you when it comes to writing the description, so don't be afraid to try them out. You can always edit what they have written, or find another friend who can write you another one.

NEXT STEPS

Create a powerful book description that sells.

- Go to becomingabestseller.com and either create a free account or log in to your existing Path to Publish
- Create a draft of your book description or let others create it for you.
- Make sure that it doesn't go beyond 200 words.
- Compare your book description with the examples that we have given above.
- Let other people read your book description and take notes.
- If you want a compelling book description, reach out to us at coaching@becomingabestseller.com and we will help you create an amazing one.

NOTES

AUTHOR BIO: THE ART OF SELLING YOU

f you're a first-time author, you have to assume that people don't know a thing about you. So how do you introduce yourself to your prospective readers? You have to create an author biography and link it to your book, or put it as part of your back cover.

So how important is an author bio really? Well, unless you're J. R. R. Tolkien, J.K. Rowling, or Stephen King, then people have no idea who you are. These authors have published a lot of bestselling books in the past, but they still put an author bio on their books' back covers. Well, technically, the bios are not for their current followers, but it's for those who are new to their genre and are not familiar with who they are. This is how important the author bio is. Remember what we said about the book description? A sentence or two about you will boost your book's legitimacy. This is your opportunity in a single paragraph to detail what you have accomplished professionally, and as an author.

So how do you write a good author bio?

I know a few first-time authors who had a hard time creating their bios. It's not that they don't know what to write; some of them don't know where to start, since they have more than a dozen accomplishments and would like to include all of them in their bio, while others are simply not used to talking about themselves.

To help you with this task, here are a few pointers on how to create a good author bio. Remember, not all author bios that you read on book covers are good. Some are terrible, and we will show you examples of both the good and the bad.

1. You have to emphasize why you are an authority on your book's subject. By listing the things that you have accomplished professionally, this can significantly increase your credibility as an author of the subject matter at hand. If you wrote a book about depression, and you are a psychiatrist, might as well mention it so that readers will know that you have experience in dealing with this sensitive subject. If you wrote a book on starting a business, also mention your experience in guiding incubator companies in the past. However, don't overstate it. Readers don't need to know all the local awards that you achieved since the 1970s, so make sure that you include the relevant ones only.

   If you are struggling to create your author bio, just remember that the main goal is to make people aware that you are an authority on the subject, and why they should listen to you.

   Now, this really depends on the genre of your book. If you're writing a thriller or mystery novel, then it's harder to actually come up with a sentence that signals direct credibility. If you have not won awards for writing in the past, then might as well concentrate on the other parts of the bio.

2. Try to include things that are interesting, but never go overboard. I have read a few bios that are interesting, and even funny ones, which further grab the attention of the readers. Remember, humor sells! You can also add interesting bits about yourself to make it sound personable.

   I know one author who has just published his first fiction book, and since it was a passion project for him, his background and career highlights being far from writing (he was a scientist), he struggled in creating his author bio since he had nothing relevant to write. But after numerous tries and a couple of tweaks, his bio came out really well! It was funny, and he even mentioned that he had won a national championship in chess, and that he could solve one Sudoku grid in less than three minutes. This was not related to his book whatsoever, but it added color to it. People got interested in his book because his personality was colorful and fun.

3. If you have a website, don't forget to mention it in your author bio. If readers found your author bio interesting, they might want to look up your website to learn more things about you, so always include it in your bio. Also, if you have written other books in the past, include them too. If they like your second book, who knows, they might even purchase your first one!

    If you take a look at other authors who have written other books in the past, they always mention their other works in their bios, most especially if that book won an award. Take Stephen King for example. This author is already a household name, but still includes his other written works in his author bio. A good bio example would be on his book IT:

"Stephen King is the author of more than fifty books, all them worldwide bestsellers. His recent work includes The Bill Hodges Trilogy..."

In just two sentences, Stephen King was able to establish that he is one of the best authors today, and has also given you the idea that he has three recent books (trilogy), which you might have not read yet (or had no idea at all that they existed). So what will you do after reading IT and you actually liked it? I don't know about you, but I will surely head to amazon. com later and purchase The Bill Hodges trilogy!

4. Name-dropping can also be done in the author bio. If you have worked with a famous person to perfect your craft in the past, or someone known in the field of your subject matter (it doesn't matter if the person's famous or not) then don't be afraid to name-drop. Some readers might recognize him and might actually buy your book because of the person you named. However, keep in mind that you have to name-drop subtly—don't be so crass about it. Most people are put off if the name-dropping is done wrong. However, there is a right way to do it.

    If, say, you appeared as a guest in a podcast of a known person, and that person called your magic realism book "enchanting", then you can include in your bio something like, "The author of the book that John Doe called enchanting..." Listeners of John Doe, the podcaster, will surely be interested in your book!

5. Lastly, keep it interesting and short. You don't want a very long author bio as people might get bored reading it. I have seen some books that have super-long author bios, and frankly, readers just graze past through them. They don't even read the entire thing! So keep your bios short and interesting. Remember, the typical number of words for the bio is more or less 200 words.

WHY IS IT IMPORTANT?

Author bios are important not only because they let the readers know more about you, but they also impact book sales.

There is such a thing called "author reputation" and this is one of the main factors why people actually buy some books. Take Tony Robbins for example. People who are into business strategies are more inclined to purchase his book knowing that it was published by Tony Robbins himself. So, letting people know who you are and what you do, will pave the way to increased book sales.

Also, if readers see that you are an authority on the topic, then the author bio is a great way to establish some authority in the subject matter. A person who has advanced degrees in Economics, and has published a book about his analyses of the stock market in the next 20 years, will be seen as an authority. If we compare this to someone who has advanced degrees in Literature, and this someone has also published a book on the same subject matter, then people won't see him on the same level of authority as the Economics grad, right?

Another sad truth is that some people will judge the content of your book based on the bio that you have written on the back cover. This is sad but true. An author bio is so much easier to read as it is just a paragraph long compared to the book, and if people find your author bio boring, or too crass, then they might just drop your book and get another one. Snap judgements happen all the time, and the author bio is no exception.

HERE ARE A FEW EXAMPLES OF BIOS:

TIM FERRISS: PERFECT BALANCE

See how his bio lists all of his relevant awards, his other works, and interesting facts about his published books (published in 30+ languages), yet he is able to keep his bio to under 200 words? All the things he has listed in his bio add to his credibility; however, he still makes it interesting to his readers.

Timothy Ferriss is a serial entrepreneur, #1 New York Times best-selling author, and angel investor/advisor (Facebook, Twitter, Evernote, Uber, and 20+ more). Best known for his rapid-learning techniques, Tim's books — The 4-Hour Work Week, The 4-Hour Body, and The 4-Hour Chef — have been published in 30+ languages. The 4-Hour Work Week has spent seven years on The New York Times bestseller list.

Tim has been featured by more than 100 media outlets including The New York Times, The Economist, TIME, Forbes, Fortune, Outside, NBC, CBS, ABC, Fox and CNN. He has guest-lectured in entrepreneurship at Princeton University since 2003. His popular blog www.fourhourblog.com has 1M+ monthly readers, and his Twitter account @tferriss was selected by Mashable as one of only five "Must-Follow" accounts for entrepreneurs. Tim's primetime TV show, The Tim Ferriss Experiment (www.upwave.com/tfx), teaches rapid-learning techniques for helping viewers to produce seemingly superhuman results in minimum time.[24]

CHERYL STRAYED: A LITTLE OVERSELLING AND A BIT CONFUSING

Though Cheryl was able to keep her author bio under 200 words, this chunk of text is confusing for some, since she included unnecessary information such as who will direct the film adaptation of her book (The film is directed by Jean-Marc Vallée and stars Reese Witherspoon, with a screenplay by Nick Hornby.) This information is not relevant to the book, and her overall bio could be 25% shorter than it is now.

Cheryl Strayed is the author of #1 New York Times bestseller WILD, the New York Times bestseller TINY BEAUTIFUL THINGS, and the novel TORCH. WILD was chosen by Oprah Winfrey as her first selection for Oprah's Book Club 2.0. WILD won a Barnes & Noble Discover Award, an Indie Choice Award, an Oregon Book Award, a Pacific Northwest Booksellers Award, and a Midwest Booksellers Choice Award, among others. The movie adaptation of WILD will be released by Fox Searchlight in December 2014. The film is directed by Jean-Marc Vallée and stars Reese Witherspoon, with a screenplay by Nick Hornby. Strayed's writing has appeared in THE BEST AMERICAN ESSAYS, the New York Times Magazine, the Washington Post Magazine, Vogue, Salon, The Missouri Review, The Sun, Tin House, The Rumpus—where she wrote the popular "Dear Sugar" advice column—and elsewhere. Strayed was the guest editor of BEST AMERICAN ESSAYS 2013 and has contributed to many anthologies. Her books have been translated into more than thirty languages around the world. She holds an MFA in fiction writing from Syracuse University and a bachelor's degree from the University of Minnesota. She lives in Portland, Oregon with her husband and their two children.[25]

DR. DAVID PERLMUTTER: STRING OF AWARDS

I do understand that if you're a doctor, you're probably very proud of your awards as you worked hard on those. But enough of bragging and listing down all the awards you got, even way back in med school. It doesn't do any good for your book, and you are only confusing the readers more. They want to know who you are as an author, not hire you based on your resume.

David Perlmutter, MD, FACN, ABIHM is a Board-Certified Neurologist and Fellow of the American College of Nutrition who received his M.D. degree from the University of Miami School of Medicine where he won the research award. Dr. Perlmutter is a frequent lecturer at symposia sponsored by such medical institutions as Columbia University, the University of Arizona, Scripps Institute, and Harvard University. He has contributed extensively to the world of medical literature, with publications appearing in The Journal of Neurosurgery, The Southern Medical Journal, Journal of Applied Nutrition, and Archives of Neurology. He is the author of: The Better Brain Book and the #1 New York Times Bestseller, Grain Brain. He is recognized internationally as a leader in the field of nutritional influences in neurological disorders. Dr. Perlmutter has been interviewed on many nationally syndicated radio and television programs, including 20/20, Larry King Live, CNN, Fox News, Fox and Friends, The Today Show, Oprah, Dr. Oz, and The CBS Early Show. In 2002 Dr. Perlmutter was the recipient of the Linus Pauling Award for his innovative approaches to neurological disorders, and in addition, was awarded the Denham Harmon Award for his pioneering work in the application of free radical science to clinical medicine. He is the recipient of the 2006 National Nutritional Foods Association Clinician of the Year Award. Dr. Perlmutter serves as Medical Advisor for The Dr. Oz Show.[26]

DR. BENJAMIN CARSON: GREAT DOCTOR BIO

On the other hand, there are good doctor bios out there. Take Dr. Carson for example. His bio focuses on his credentials that his readers would care about, and everything that he has written can be understood by most people.

Dr. Benjamin Carson is a Professor of Neurosurgery, Plastic Surgery, Oncology, and Pediatrics, and the Director of Pediatric Neurosurgery at Johns Hopkins Medical Institutions. He is also the author of four bestselling books—Gifted Hands, Think Big, The Big Picture, and Take the Risk. He serves on the boards of the Kellogg Company, Costco, and the Academy of Achievement, among others, and is an Emeritus Fellow of the Yale Corporation.

He and his wife, Candy, co-founded the Carson Scholars Fund (www.carsonscholars.org), a 501(c)3 established to counteract America's crisis in education by identifying and rewarding academic role models in the fourth through eleventh grades, regardless of race, creed, religion and socio-economic status, who also demonstrate humanitarian qualities. There are over 4800 scholars in forty-five states. Ben and Candy are the parents of three grown sons and reside in Baltimore County, Maryland.[27]

LYNN VINCENT: LESS IS MORE!

Indeed, author bios can be less than 100 words—heck, it can even be less than 60 words, yet make an impact. Look at Lynn's bio below. She has written a very short bio, but it tells a lot about her (being a co-author of 10 books, which have sold 12 million copies). Only an established author can sell more than 12 million copies, so this statement adds to her credibility and legitimacy, big time!

·

Lynn Vincent is the New York Times best-selling writer of Heaven Is for Real and Same Kind of Different As Me. The author or coauthor of ten books, Lynn has sold 12 million copies since 2006. She worked for eleven years as a writer and editor at the national news biweekly WORLD magazine and is a U.S. Navy veteran.[28]

MICHAEL LEWIS: SHORT AND UNDERSELLS

This author challenges Lynn Vincent's bio in the shortness department, and clearly, Michael Lewis won. With only 39 words, his bio clearly undersells how brilliant a writer he is. Lewis is a known author, and even though you are a popular author, don't assume that everyone knows you by just listing the titles of your other works. Some of his works have been turned into films already, but I know a few people who have not even seen the movie adaptations of his books, more so read the book versions.

Michael Lewis, the author of Boomerang, Liar's Poker, The New New Thing, Moneyball, The Blind Side, Panic, Home Game and The Big Short, among other works, lives in Berkeley, California, with his wife, Tabitha Soren, and their three children.[29]

Create a relatable author bio that people will love.

- Go to becomingabestseller.com and either create a free account or log in to your existing Path to Publish
- Create a draft author bio or let others create it for you.
- Make sure that it doesn't go beyond 200 words.
- Compare your author bio with the examples that we have shown above.
- Let other people read your author bio and take notes.
- If you want a compelling author bio, reach out to us at coaching@becomingabestseller.com and we will help you create an amazing one.

AMAZON BOOK PAGE: EVERYTHING YOUR READERS NEED TO KNOW

At this point, you already have the final copy of your book, ready to be uploaded on Amazon's KDP (Kindle Direct Publishing). This is it! You're now one step away from publishing your book and letting millions of people read it. This is the final step in officially becoming an author.

The Amazon book page is what readers first see when they browse your book. This is basically your book's "homepage", so it should have all the information about your book that is relevant to the reader. Let's go over all the parts of the Amazon book page to better prepare you with the things that you will need to gather in order to create a compelling book page.

You need to be organized at this point. Creating a folder in your computer with all the required files is a great way to ensure that you don't miss anything. First, you need a nice book design. If you have already had your book cover designed during the previous sections, then you are already done. Save that picture in your folder, ready to be uploaded to your book page.

Next, you have to write your book title and subtitle, include your foreword if you have any, and the two (or three) different formats that you have available (ebook, paperback, and audiobook).

Paste the book description that you have created into your book page. Read it once again to make sure that there are no errors whatsoever. Even a little error will turn readers off, so make sure it's error-free.

Get a copy of the author bio that you created and paste it in the author bio field. Readers usually click on the author's bio link if they find the book description interesting, so make sure that your author bio is short and interesting as well. Who knows? You might be able to start a small following because of your funny side and quirkiness. Also, if you have a website, you can include that in your author bio. This is free marketing, folks! Free, organic marketing. If people find you interesting, they will definitely click on your website link, and if you have your other works there, or perhaps, events that you have lined up, then people might come! I know one author who put his link to his scheduler in his bio, and he said that he got a 15% increase in his bookings. That's a 15% increase for doing nothing at all. He just pasted a link to his profile, and it didn't even take him 10 seconds to do it! Take advantage of this opportunity and don't forget to include links about you or your other works.

Next, you have to enter the product details of your book, such as the number of pages, the dimensions of your book, ISBN number, the publication date, the publisher, and perhaps the most important part, you have to select the categories where your book belongs. This part is crucial in determining your bestseller status. Remember that you only need to become a bestseller in one category to become a bestselling author, so you have to pick the categories that will best apply to your book. Do not pick easy categories that are pretty far from your book's theme just so you can become number one. If your book is about self-help, and you categorized it under history, no one will be able to search for your book, so this won't be beneficial for your book at all. So, make sure that you pick the right categories.

Lastly, and probably the most important part of the book page, is the reviews part. At this point, prior to the publishing of your book, you don't need to worry about this yet. Just focus on uploading your book right now to KDP. It's understandable that when you first upload your book to KDP, you won't have reviews for that particular book yet. It's new, so you have to allow some time for readers to search for your book, read it, and leave a review. We will give you tips in the future sections of this book on how to gather more reviews if you want to speed things up, because technically, the more reviews you have for your book, the better the sales. Think of it as a product that you are going to buy. If there are two similar items on the marketplace, and the first product has 20 good reviews, and the other has no reviews at all, which product would you buy? Definitely the one with reviews. People love social proof, and this also applies to books on Amazon.

NEXT STEPS

Be organized when you upload content to your Amazon book page.

- Go to becomingabestseller.com and either create a free account or log in to your existing Path to Publish
- Time for a list. Have the following in a folder:
  - Book title and subtitle
  - Book description
  - Author bio
  - Link to your website
  - Product details
  - Categories for your book
  - Reviews
- Upload each one and make sure you are uploading the right content (your bio should go under author bio)
- Ask us at coaching@becomingabestseller.com if you have questions about your book's details, or if you need help in creating your Amazon book page.

NOTES

PROFIT

THE

MARKETING:

BOOK

GROWTH

HACKING

Here we are now, at the most dreaded part of becoming a bestseller. This is the make or break part after you have published your book, and this will determine whether your book will become a bestseller or not. Publishing is not enough, as you still need to market it to reach more readers. We might have discussed some techniques in the earlier section, but in this section, we are going to dive deeper into the different marketing methods that you can use for your book.

The first website that we will share with you is eReleases (https://ereleases.com). This website works wonders when it comes to press releases and will help you get more exposure for your book. Press releases are important for a brand or an initiative. The more press releases you send out, the more chances that people will see what you have to offer. However, it's not just about publishing any kind of press release on the internet. The quality of press releases also matters. If, say, two different companies are doing press releases at the same time, and company A posted three press releases to high PR sites such as CNN, Yahoo!, and Wall Street Journal, while on the other hand, company B posted 30 press releases to small-time blogs and news sources. Which of the two do you think would gain more exposure? The answer is pretty obvious.

eReleases is also by far the cheapest and fastest way to get media coverage. It is the cheapest website that we have found which offers excellent services for a small price (compared to other similar services). Also, we have tested this website and they work wonders. They are a legit company, and they also have a partnership with PR Newswire, so you can be assured that they do not just send their press releases to their own private network, but tap other journalists as well, who might pick up your story.

FREE ORGANIC GROWTH STRATEGY

FB GROUPS

In today's world, we must admit that social media sites are the kings of marketing. They generate billions of dollars per quarter in advertising, and they do this because of the leverage that they have, compared to other sites offering ads placement: they have millions of active users every day, you included. They even have apps and millions of people have downloaded their applications, which means you can reach potential readers even faster, more like real time. When you were browsing your own Facebook home page, did you see little boxes of advertisements for air humidifiers, courses online, etc.? Think about it. If that advertisement reached you, then you also have the potential to reach other users by using Facebook.

We know that these ads were created for a fee. You cannot post an ad for free in social media sites, as that is how they earn their money. However, there are other ways on how you can market your book without paying a single cent. This is what we call organic marketing. In layman's terms, organic marketing is the method of marketing wherein people find your advertised product over time, without having to pay for advertising.

One method that is free in Facebook is by joining groups that are focused on your agenda. So, since you would like to market your book on Facebook, you need to join groups that do book promotion. The reach might not be as wide as doing a paid advertisement, but hey, anything for free marketing, right? The challenge is finding good groups with active members in them. Doing a quick Facebook search will probably generate a few good groups, but there are other groups out there that are beyond Facebook's reach. Either they are closed groups, or they just don't appear in the search results. Not finding these groups is a missed opportunity for you, so we have gathered a list of 150 groups that you can join and connect with. These groups are classified, depending on the book genre, and the type of promotion that they do. You just have to make sure that once you join, you follow their guidelines, as some groups are very strict about it, and they don't care if they lose a member by kicking you out once you violate their terms.

The way to really benefit from these Facebook groups is to post to all of them on your launch date. Sure, trickle promotion might get you a few likes and a few link visits, but if you want to feel a spike on your book sales and Amazon book page visits, you have to post the promotion on your book launch date. Now imagine posting to all these 150 groups at the same time. Right after you post your promotion, two people per group see it, visit your link, and buy your book. That's already a total of 300 book sales in the first hour of your book launch! Think of the other users who would actually see your book at a later time since they have not checked their Facebook apps yet. The numbers might double, or even triple! This is the power of free, organic marketing through Facebook groups.

POSTING ON FB AND IG

Approximately 30 days before your selected launch date, you should have started doing a little marketing on the side. You can do this via Facebook and Instagram, as posting to these sites is free and can generate a lot of followers for your book even before its official release date.

Pick 30 of your favorite quotes from your book, create amazing designs and release one quote per day. People on Facebook, especially on Instagram, like quotes laid out beautifully on pretty designs. If you are an Instagram user, you probably have liked a post before because of how aesthetically pleasing the design was. It showed that the user took some time to design the post and by liking it, you wanted to show your support. Same goes with your posts. There are many tools on the internet that have drag and drop features if you don't know how to use photoshop. You don't even need to be a computer whiz to be able to create nice designs.

Canva (https://www.canva.com) is one of the sites that offers this kind of service. You can create an account for free, and they also have upgrades if you want to take your designs to the next level, but the basic ones should be enough. It's fairly easy to manipulate designs in Canva, since every element can be changed. If you want a specific background color, you can also use color hexes to get the right shade that you're aiming for. A background design is also possible if you want to have hexagonal shapes or something else. Resizing the element is also easy with Canva, as a you just need to select the element, then drag the corners to make it smaller.

Another option, if you want to do the designs on your mobile phone, is to download the application called Over. This app is available on both iOS and Android, so everyone should be able to download it. If you go to Instagram and you see designs that are so beautiful you thought they were made by professionals, don't be shocked when you learn that they were made through the app Over. It's a very versatile application and it utilizes drag and drop, and pinch and zoom features to adjust the elements of your design. Due to the small screen features of mobile phones, some find it hard to actually tinker with the design, so it is recommended that you use a device with a bigger screen such as a tablet or an iPad. If you don't have a tablet or an iPad, you can still use

Over on your computer by downloading an emulator such as Bluestacks, and accessing the app through it.

Once you have created 30 designs, as mentioned, you have to post one quote per day on both your Facebook and Instagram. This is pretty tedious, considering that you are doing a lot of things already with the publishing and the marketing of your book. Again, we live in the 21st century, and as the saying goes, "there is an app for that". Yes! There are a lot of scheduling apps that post automatically on your social media pages, once you have given them permission. One site is Hootsuite (http://hootsuite.com), and the other one is Postcron (https://postcron.com). These tools are free to use, but they also offer an upgrade so that you can schedule more posts and link more social media sites if you need to. However, the free plans should be enough to get you going. Now, before you schedule a post, you need to research on the best times that you should post on Facebook and Instagram. Though Facebook owns Instagram, both of these sites cater for different markets, so it is essential to know when is that "golden hour" when you need to post your content for maximum exposure.

For Instagram, you also need to know about hashtags so that you can maximize your reach to Instagram users. You can also research on this by looking at other posts similar to yours, or hire an Instagram hashtag researcher on Upwork for guaranteed results. Once you get this right, the results are astonishing. You can even gain a little following on Instagram for your book, and do promotions there!

FACEBOOK ADVERTISING

We have all heard about Facebook advertising. We know that this platform is what companies are using now, be it a small, medium, or a large-sized company. It is an exceptional tool that millions of people are registered to, and they have guaranteed active users that check the site every day, so it's a marketing gold mine. However, for those who have not tried Facebook advertising, and have just read tutorials off the internet, it can be quite confusing. For those who have tried it in the past, but never had guidance from an expert on Facebook ads, you might have spent thousands of dollars on it, but never had amazing results. So, it is no surprise that, for most people, Facebook advertising can be as intimidating as hell.

What's troublesome is, the more research that you do, the more overwhelmed you feel because of the various guides and websites that claim they are the best growth hack, and that people should follow them to achieve great results. All of them. FB ads have a lot of options to choose from, I agree, but all you have to do is be familiar with the platform, and soon that overwhelming feeling of confusion will be gone. Just like any new tech, you need to know how it works to fully use it. When you purchased your very first smartphone, did you already know how to use it? Maybe you knew how to operate the basic features of it, but after tinkering with it for a while, you probably went, "Oh, so that's how you screenshot," or maybe, "Oh, there is a way to open the camera from the volume rocker." Things like these, you don't exactly know all at once. You learn some of the things along the way, and that's ok.

Facebook ads is a great way to invest time and money. Though it is quite confusing to begin with, what's great about it is you will have immense control over your ads' customization. Would you like to target male vegan parents who love skiing? How about adolescent football fans in the Manhattan area? The ads are fully customizable, and you will be able to reach your target market effectively when you use this filtering feature.

Now, for the cost; Facebook ads is still pretty cheap compared to other ad serving companies such as Google Adwords. If your ads are given a high relevance score, which means that your ads are very relevant for your target audience, Facebook rewards you by lowering your Cost Per Click (CPC). CPC in layman's terms, is the cost that you will have to spend for each click that people do on your ad. If your CPC is $0.40, then whenever people see your ad, and they click on it because they are interested in it, Facebook charges you $0.40 for that.

So, how do you create amazing Facebook ads? It's pretty simple and we are going to give you only eight steps to achieve that winning ad of yours.

First, you have to develop your strategy. Before you start tinkering with your Facebook ads manager, you have to first develop a strategy on paper. Without a solid strategy, you will be creating ads that will target just about everyone else, and you will be confused with all the options that are laid before you.

You need to ask yourself the following:

- What products and services am I going to promote?
- Who is my target market?
- Are they going to be a cold or warm audience?
- How will these people use my products?
- What are their objectives? What is their pain?
- At what stage of my funnel are they in?
- What is the ultimate goal of the campaign I am creating?
- Is my end goal to get more leads, traffic to my site, sales, brand awareness, or something else?

Second, you have to choose your objective. This part is crucial, as Facebook will optimize your advertisements based on what you chose. In some instances, Facebook will lower your CPC based on what objective you chose. The following are the available objectives to choose from:

- Brand awareness
- Reach
- Traffic
- Engagement

- App installs
- Video views
- Lead generation
- Messages
- Conversions
- Catalogue Sales
- Store Visits

You have to select the correct objective so that Facebook can optimize and improve your results. If you are promoting your book, and you want people to buy your book, then you have to choose conversions instead of something else. If Marvel, for example, released a trailer for their new movie, they would want to select video views as their objective.

Third, you have to select the right target market for your ad. By now, you should have a clear idea of which audience you want to target for your book. Are you targeting local residents, maybe within the 25 mile radius? Or maybe an entire state? Or perhaps, people from your state who are interested in your book topic? This is where the customization of the ad starts. You can be as flexible as you can with your ads, and be a specific as you can be, but remember, the more specified your target is, the lesser the reach is. If you are going to target "Everyone in New York who is interested in crypto currency," you will probably get 10 million people for your reach. However, if you specify it to, "Males between 18 and 23 in the Upper Manhattan area who are interested in Bitcoin," then you would probably get about 100,000 only. This is the difference when it comes to specifying the target market.

Fourth, you have to select your ad level. This is where you will instruct Facebook where to place your ads on their site. Do you want it shown on desktops only, and just on feeds and as suggested videos? You can be as specific as possible. I have seen one mobile phone app which has only targeted mobile phone users, because it totally made sense. Though they are ostracizing the desktop users, typing in the name of the app on your phone is another step and people might lose their interest along the way. So, by targeting mobile phone users only, these users simply need to click on the link and they will be redirected to the App store or Play store. Think about these things when you are choosing your ad level. It's not about reaching everyone who uses Facebook, but the clever placement of ads all over the site will help you reach more targeted individuals. I have also seen a coffee shop ad on "mobile phone only" as they are targeting people on the go; institutions that offer courses on desktop only as they listen and learn on their computers, not on their mobile phones. You get the drift.

Fifth, you have to set your budget. This is where you need to be realistic. You can either choose to have a daily budget or a lifetime budget. Daily budget, as self-explanatory as it can be, is your daily cap for the amount that you are willing to spend for your ads per day. Lifetime budget is your budget for the entire campaign—if the money runs out, your campaign ends. If you set $20 as your daily budget, then your ad will run until your daily budget runs out. It could be less than $20 depending on your CPC, but it will never go over your $20 budget. Remember, there are peak hours as to when Facebook is very active for your desired location. Say, you chose New York for your location on your ad. People in that location are usually active during business hours and at night time. If you start your advertisement at 3:00 in the morning, then your budget will run longer due to inactivity. But if you post during peak hours, and your ad is really interesting, your $20 might just last for a few hours.

You also have to choose what you're bidding on for the ads. Will it be clicks or impressions? We have discussed what clicks are, but impressions are defined as ad views. So people can view your ads, but not click on it. Again, it depends on your objective at this point. Always go back to the strategy that you developed in step one.

Sixth, you have to select an ad format. There are five different ad formats that Facebook is offering:

- Carousel ads, wherein you can create an ad with two or more scrollable images or videos
- Single image ads
- Single Video ads
- Slideshow ads
- Collection ads, wherein the images open to a full screen mobile experience.

You can select which ad type is best for you; however, we do recommend video ads and carousel ads as they tend to have higher engagements and CTR (Click Through Rate; the percentage of users who click on the link).

Seventh, you have to include the link that you are promoting and the text that the people will see when your ad pops up. This is perhaps the most important part as this is basically your frontend. This is what users see and decide, in a few seconds, if they will click on your ad or not. It's the creative section, and your job is to make your ad enticing enough so that people will stop and click on your ad, while speed-scrolling through their Facebook homepage. Some people hire copywriters who are good at creating catchy ads to create the narrative part for them. It's because this part is actually your ticket for people to click on your ad. It doesn't matter if your ad is perfect in the backend. If the creative part of your ad sucks, no one will click on it.

Eighth, you have to monitor your campaigns. If you have created various ads, you will be able see at this point which ads are working, and which aren't. Don't just create ads and forget about them. This is not how it works. You should monitor them after creating them to ensure that the ads are running perfectly well. If there are ads that have higher than normal CPCs, your ads might not be optimized the way they should be, so you should check this out, or maybe you need to tweak it a bit to find the perfect balance.

NEXT STEPS

Create an unstoppable Facebook ad.

- Go to becomingabestseller.com and either create a free account or log in to your existing Path to Publish
- Sign up for a package with eReleases.com
- In a spreadsheet, create your 30 quotes and hire a designer for it
- Sign up for automatic posting via Hootsuite or Postcron
- Develop your Facebook ad strategy
- Set up your ads correctly, based on your goals and targets
- If you want guidance in creating your ads, or if you want for us to create your ads for you, contact us at coaching@becomingabestseller.com and we will do it for you.

NOTES

AMAZON ADVERTISING: FIGHTING OFF COMPETITORS

ust like Facebook ads, Amazon also has their own branch of advertising which is called the Amazon Marketing Services (AMS). We are well aware how crowded the Amazon market is. Lots of sellers, and lots of options to choose from. But how do you stand out from this over-saturated market of just about anything?

They have a solution though, which is to advertise your book on their site so that it shows up on the search results, or even next to a competitor's book page! How amazing (and evil) is that? AMS is more effective, according to data, compared to Facebook ads or Google Adwords because basically, you are already advertising on a marketplace where people go to buy something. People are already there, have logged in, and are ready to check out the next book they are going to read.

So what exactly is AMS? It is very similar to Facebook and Google ads, wherein you pay Amazon a certain amount every time a customer clicks on your book. Don't fret though, as we are talking about $0.05 cents to $0.45 per click, so it's not that big of a deal.

Before you start your AMS ads, make sure that you have already uploaded your book into your own Amazon KDP account. Some authors, who go through a middleman or other self-publishing company, will not have access to their KDPs since they don't have access to their accounts (not unless your publishing company gives you access). So better make sure that your book is in your KDP account, since Amazon only allows people to promote books that they own.

There are basically two types of campaigns for AMS: Sponsored Products and Product Display Ads, and the campaign type that you choose will depend on your end goal. Sponsored ads are keyword-targeted ads, so whenever someone searches for a keyword that your book has, your book will display on the search results. You can even select a date range for your ads, depending on how long you want your AMS ads to run. On the other hand, product display ads are interest-targeted ads and can display on related products that people have searched for. This is when you can make your book appear on your competitor's page! A bit evil, but hey, this is a dog-eat-dog world, and marketing is a very competitive sector of the business world.

Two options are available for the targeting, unlike Facebook, wherein you can fully customize your ads based on the filters that you choose. With AMS, you can only select a few filters for your targeting. If you are not super-technical and are not familiar with the targeting aspect of an AMS campaign, then you can opt for automatic targeting. This way, you can let Amazon choose the targeting for you. However, if you have a few keywords up your sleeve, you can do manual targeting as well. This way, you can select the keywords based on what Amazon suggested, or you can input your own keywords on the ad campaign.

As you can see, AMS is not as flexible and customizable as Facebook ads. Their difference lies in the intent of the customers. With Facebook, you need to fully customize the ad since the people you are showing it to are on the site to connect socially with their friends, and have no intention of buying books at the moment. However, for Amazon, people are already there to buy something, so you just need to maneuver them to your book page so that they will buy your book instead of your competitor's.

EBOOK SITES (PROMOTING)

Remember the list of Facebook groups that we gave you for the book promotion? Luckily, it's not only limited to Facebook, as there are tons of sites that offer the same service. We offered 150+ Facebook groups that you could join and promote your book to, but how does 250+ book promotion sites sound to you?! Great, right? Some of these sites allow you to post for free, but for the others, they require payment to be listed on their site. What's good about these services is they have an email list that they can send an email blast to, and reach millions of people.

You have to do this together with your Facebook and Instagram post, as you need to do it 30 days before your book launch. Should you decide to do the free sites, that's ok too, but if you want a total boost, you can also opt for the paid ones. What you need to do is email them a month before your launch date and tell them when your book is launching. That's it! On the day of your book launch, they will all send an email blast to their listserv and this will give you a spike in Kindle downloads. They have millions on their list so this will certainly move you up to the top tier in your Amazon book category. Take note, though, that some of these sites require that you have five to ten Amazon reviews to start with, so if you don't have the required reviews yet, you can definitely skip them and get back to them later once you have the reviews.

QUORA STRATEGY

Not everyone knows about Quora. It is a site that is barely visited by many, however, if you do a simple Google search on any query that you have, you will see that Quora actually ranks high in the search results. It is not a surprise though, as Quora is classified as a question and answer website, and the question you asked has probably been answered in Quora already. But how is this relevant in your book's marketing? Quite relevant, I must say. Though Quora is not used to promote books, you can subtly do it through your author bio.

If, say, your book is about marriage counseling, we can assume that you're an expert when it comes to this topic. When creating a Quora account, you can select marriage counseling and as many of the topics that are similar or close to it as possible, so that all the questions that you will get are about it. Once you have created an account, you will see the recommended list of questions, and since you're an expert on this topic, you can fire away answers like a pro.

But before you get too excited and start answering questions, you have to first fill out your profile. This is the most important part, as you want people to recognize you as someone who is credible to answer the questions you're answering, and to hopefully redirect them to your Amazon book page eventually. The profile requires you to fill in your educational and work backgrounds, as well as a short description about yourself. You can put a one-sentence description, but at the end of it, make sure that you include the link to your website or your Amazon book. Whenever you answer questions, your description gets displayed on the top part of your answer, so this is actually a good and effective way to deliver traffic to your book or your site.

If you are just starting with Quora and your book promotion, answer questions aggressively. Take time to browse all the available questions in the recommendations, and don't just give short answers. Make sure that you give out long, well-thought-out answers, as this will determine whether people will check your profile, and click on your link. If your answers are super-short, people might think that you don't really like what you're doing and that you are just in Quora to market something. Your answers have to be helpful to people so they browse your profile and check your link out.

Now, if you are going to put a link to your website or your book, make sure that you track these links by shortening it with services such as bit.ly, so that you can keep track of how effective your Quora campaign is. You can keep track as to how many people click on it per day, week, or month, and adjust your Quora strategy accordingly. Set a certain number of clicks over a period of time. Say, if your goal is 40 clicks per week, and the number of clicks dips below that number, then answer more questions until you are satisfied with the numbers. Remember, the more questions you answer, the better exposure you get.

There is also a section in your profile that says "Knows About..." and this tallies all the topics that you have answered. If you answered 100 questions on marriage counseling, 75 on psychology, 10 on baking, and 5 on plumbing, then people will know that you are an authority on marriage counseling and psychology, but not on baking and plumbing. This helps you build your credibility in Quora as well, and people might just purchase your book because they have seen how good your answers are, and that you always have a call to action in your answers and profile.

BLOG AND PODCAST STRATEGY

This section talks about the strategies you can adopt for both blogs and podcasts. Blogs and podcasts cater for a certain niche that most news outlets do not cover. They also have a loyal following, and most of their tribe or subscribers have their notifications set up so that whenever there's a new show or post, they are the first ones to read or listen to it. It's amazing how these groups, though small, are very active, and being featured in one of their stories will give you the boost that you need.

First, we have the blogs. It's very easy to create one, and some sites even host blogs for free, so you have to be very careful as to what blog sites you use to promote your book. They might claim that they have thousands of readers, but the truth is, they don't have a hundred followers. Remember, anyone can claim anything on the internet. Big blog sites have an email list, and they notify their followers whenever a new post is live. So just to be sure that what you'll get is a legit list of the top blogs out there, what you need to do is simple: search it on Google. Type in the search box, "top 10 blogs on X", where x is your topic, such as cryptocurrency, marriage counseling, and so on. You will then get the top 10 blogs in a list, probably compiled on a website, and all you need to do is visit the linked blogs there and contact them. Whether it's via email or through their contact form, it doesn't matter as long as you reach them.

The good news is, we have an effective template just for you. This template is what you can copy and paste, you just have to change some of the details, and you can send it away. Once you are done with the first list from the Google search results, you are not done yet. Open the second one and do the same thing you did on the first one. Do not stop unless you have exhausted all the lists. Change your keywords in Google search if you want to, so that you can get different results.

For the podcasts, it's a different method as you don't need to do a Google search. You just need to go to https://www.ra-dioguestlist.com/ and click on the "See New Radio Interview Guest Requests" link to see all the podcast requests for the day. Each day you will see about five new podcast requests, and though not all podcasts can be applied to you, you can wait for another day when there are suitable podcasts for your topic. Should you decide to check out the available podcasts for the previous day, you can pay them a certain fee to upgrade your account. However, if you want to stay on the free plan, you can just check on the page every day, until one pops along.

Once you have found a possible podcast topic, click on it and read their guidelines. Read the fine print as well, and complete all the requirements. They will either want to be contacted via email or through their site, so follow accordingly.

Just a note though, the podcasts that you find via RadioGuestList are small-time podcasts with only a small following. If you want to be featured in big podcasts, you can use the same method as you did on the blogs. Do a Google search on the top 10 podcasts for your topic or niche and send the template that we will provide you with.

NEXT STEPS

Time to further expand your marketing campaign.

- Go to becomingabestseller.com and either create a free account or log in to your existing Path to Publish
- Pick what type of Amazon ads would work best for you.
  - Sponsored Products
  - Product Display Ads
- Sign up with the ebook promoting sites that we provided
- Create your Quora profile and start answering questions aggressively
- Research on the top 10 blogs and podcasts in your field/niche
- If you need help with your Amazon ads, or need help on how to contact the celebrities in your niche, reach out to us at coaching@becomingabestseller.com

REVIEWS:

THE BIGGEST

SOCIAL PROOF

YOU'LL NEED

Now, this is the part where we talk about your book's reviews. As we have mentioned, this could be the make or break part of your Amazon book page. People like to see social proof, and they buy more from sellers who have more reviews for their products. In some customer-centric marketplaces such as eBay, whenever you search for a product, you will see that the ones on top of the list are the products with so many reviews and verified purchases. The reason is because consumers see product A with 15 reviews and product B with no reviews at all, so they purchase product A over and over again. Having the reviews actually creates some sort of security blanket for them.

The same goes for your book. If readers see that you have a lot of reviews, and we're not just talking about star reviews on your book, but good reviews with well-thought-out written comments, then this would encourage more people to buy your book.

So how do you get more reviews for your book to start with? We're not talking about fake reviews as Amazon detects IP addresses, so you cannot buy your own book and create great reviews yourself. That is illegal, and there is no joy in doing that. It doesn't feel right either. Yes, you have amazing reviews, but knowing that it was you who wrote all those reviews all along, just doesn't boost your morale as an author. What you can do instead is to start with your inner circle. Yes, we're talking about your close friends, your co-workers, your family, and your neighbors. Anyone you could think of really, to whom you can talk about your book, give a copy to, and ask for a review.

Make a list of 100 people in a spreadsheet. Jot down their phone numbers and email addresses, and ask them if you can send them a free copy of your ebook in exchange for a review. Most of your friends would probably say yes, and some would say no, but that's ok. Just keep looking for more friends to whom you can send your ebook. Most of them would probably say no because they are busy, and don't have time to read a book, but if you insist, you can actually just tell them that they just need to read a few chapters, and give you a star rating as that is the most important thing. The comment rating is not that important if they really don't have the time to do it. Tell them that once they finish reading your book, they can always go back to their rating and change it. This way, you have your ratings on Amazon as close to your launch date as possible.

If you don't want to create a list of your friends and start calling them one by one, then you can opt for the easier way, which is to post it on social media. Go to your Facebook and tell your Facebook friends that you have an upcoming book. Ask them who is willing to get a free copy of your book in exchange for a review on Amazon, and once someone comments on your post, send them the copy through Facebook Messenger. This might not be as personal as contacting them via phone and asking them if they are willing to read your book, but this method is also effective in getting a few reviews from your social media friends.

BOOK REVIEW SITES

You might be the type of person who doesn't want to bother his or her friends at all. That's fine, too. We understand that you might have personal reasons why you don't want to share your masterpiece with your close friends. If this is the case, then you can opt for companies that offer book review services. There are tons of websites out there, and you can choose which company to hire for your book review project. We, however, do recommend Happy Book Reviews (https://happybookreviews.com) and Reading Deals (https://read-ingdeals.com).

These two websites offer unique solutions to your book review problems. No need to gather up friends and follow them up for your book reviews. All you need to do is purchase their services, and you can forget about the rest. Depending on the package that you will purchase, these two companies have email lists of their own. Once your order goes through, they will include your book in their newsletter, and a copy of your book will be sent out to their pool of reviewers who have also worked on similar book genres as yours. There will be a total of 10 to 50 reviewers who will be able to download your book, depending on the package that you bought, and you just have to wait for a week or two for all the reviews to come in.

Just a few notes about this service though (and you can also read this through their Frequently Asked Questions section). First, these two companies do not guarantee positive reviews. It doesn't mean that since you paid them money, that they owe it to you to give you positive reviews. It doesn't work that way. You pay them for their readers to read your book and leave honest reviews. If your book sucks, then your reviews will suck as well.

Second, they do not guarantee that you will have 10 reviews, 15 reviews, or even 50 reviews when you purchase their package. Even though it says that they will send it to 50 reviewers, you are not guaranteed to get 50 reviews. Yes, it is true that they will send it to 50 of their reviewers, however, they have stipulated in their clause that not all of them will be reviewing your book and only those who are choosing to review your book in exchange for a free copy will leave a review. The only good thing about this is if you avail yourself of their services, you can be assured that these two companies will get your book to the right people. If they don't like your book, they might leave a bad review. If they like it, then it will be all smiles for you and your career as an author. This method is purely legal with Amazon as you are not technically buying reviews. You are paying people to read your book and leave a review (or not).

GOODREADS

If you are not comfortable with placing an order on these sites, and would like to do it the hard way and pick the reviewers yourself, then there is another option on how to gather your precious book reviews. There is a website called Goodreads. Goodreads, according to the internet, "is a social cataloging website that allows individuals to freely search its database of books, annotations, and reviews. Users can sign up and register books to generate library catalogs and reading lists. They can also create their own groups of book suggestions, surveys, polls, blogs, and discussions."[30] This means that this site is an author's dream site. Registered members of Goodreads share and discuss books among themselves and they also have a review section, though its format is different from the ones we have discussed in the past.

Once you have registered, you now have access to the top 100 reviewers of the site. What's great about this site is you can filter the reviewers by location. If you just want to see local reviewers, then you can opt for your country only, however, if you want to see the top reviewers worldwide, then you can also choose "The World" for your filter. Apart from the location filter, you can also see which reviewers are at the top for the past year, or those in the past week, depending on your preferences.

Once you have chosen the right filter for you, you can now see the top 100 reviewers based on your search criteria. If you take a look at their information, these reviewers are pretty serious about their reviewing job, and they read about one book every three days, despite having day jobs on the side. These people are bibliophiles and they read books out of passion, not because of recognition. This is why it is so much harder to please these reviewers, because basically, they have read almost all kinds of books, and have touched all niches and genres available.

What you need to do is start from the top and look at your list. Start with reviewer number one on the list and visit their profile. You will see a little snippet about the reviewer, the types of books they love to read, and their interests. If you see that the author likes sci-fi novels about aliens, you are not going to approach them, telling them that you have a romance novel for them to review. That is just absurd. You know that this reviewer doesn't like these kinds of novels at all, and you won't expect them to give something they don't enjoy reading a good review. This may not happen though, as these reviewers are objective about their reviews, but remember—liking or not liking a book is something subjec-tive. What you like might not be pleasant for someone else, and the same goes for these reviewers. They are only human after all.

So, what you can do is search for a reviewer who loves to read books in your genre. If your book is on self-help, go look for someone who enjoys self-help books. The list is composed of 100 reviewers, and there are a few of them in there, you just need to find the right person. Check their websites too, if they have it listed on their Goodreads profile. Normally, their websites are packed with information about their book review process, and most of them prefer to be contacted through their websites. Though you can use the Goodreads platform to message them, it still doesn't hurt if you check their websites to see if they have a contact form or application form for you to fill out.

As mentioned, their websites usually have information on their review policies. Check to see what their rating system is, and see if they have preferences on the books that they review. Some reviewers prefer paperbacks, and if that is the case, don't skimp and send them a paperback copy of your book. They oftentimes post the books that they enjoy on their social media, so this is additional organic traffic for you.

Again, some of them do this for the love of reading, while others do this for a fee. If you are going to email a reviewer, make sure that you ask if they are doing it for a fee, if it is not stipulated in their website already. This way, you know how much it is to have them read your review, and you can arrange for the payment with them personally.

Apart from the individuals who do book reviews, there are also groups within Goodreads that are open to the public. These groups are informal ones, and the members there share books with each other. Before joining one, make sure that you read their policies, and follow them religiously. Don't violate their policies as they may call you out with a slap on the wrist, or worse, ban you from the group. The members of the group usually share with each other good books that they have read. If book promotion is permitted, you can post your book and ask them who would like to read and leave a review for your piece. Wait for them to actually reply to your original thread, and don't repost it if no one replies to your query, as this is considered spamming, then just move on to the next group. There are some secret groups within

Goodreads as well, but you need to be invited into the group to be able to join it. If you are new to Goodreads, then open groups are enough for you to get started with.

KEYWORDS WITH PUBLISHER ROCKET

Now we are going to discuss a vital tool that will help you in marketing your product, and reaching out more to other readers. The world is now run by keywords. About three billion of the world's population have smartphones, and they all have accessed the internet at some point. People use search engines for just about everything, this is why whenever you ask a person something, which they don't know the answer to, they say, "Google it". It is being used frequently as a verb to the point that this company's name has been recently entered in the Cambridge English Dictionary with the definition, "to search for something on the internet using the Google search engine (= computer program that finds information)".

We have become dependent on the internet so much, and we use keyword searches even for mundane tasks. Things like, "baked macaroni recipe", "zombie movie with child and train", etc. We don't ask the internet with complete questions, that would be absurd. We use keywords to trigger certain search results. This way, we can get the answers we are looking for within a few seconds.

Your potential readers do the same for their book searches. They search for "business book for CEOs", "cryptocurrency guide for beginners", "marriage counseling books for rocky relationships", "book on happiness", and so on. They use keywords all the time, and if you hit the right keywords on your book title and description, your book will appear more on search results than your competitors.

This is why the tool Publisher Rocket is important for you as an author. When creating your title, subtitle, and book description, you cannot just type words that you think are cool or highfalutin. If nobody uses those words in search engines, then you are doomed. If people search for "critic" instead of "iconoclast", and you used "iconoclast" in your book title, nobody will ever find your book through search. This is just how it works.

We do recommend that you download this program for your book's sake. Publisher Rocket gives you a glimpse of how the backend works, and how many searches are being done for a certain keyword, so you know if this keyword is being used frequently by people.

By using this tool, you can either go two ways. First, you can use high target keywords in your book title and description. You probably saw that keyword A has about 30,000 searches per month, so you know that this is a good one. You can fight your way to the top using that keyword, however it will be tough. If you saw that the number of competitors for this was about 5000, then you have to fight 5,000 competitors just so you can reach the top spot for this keyword. It's going be tough, and I am not going to lie. It's good though since it's a high target keyword, and 30,000 is 30,000. However, knowing that you are going to fight tooth and nail with 5,000 other competitors is not worth it. When it comes to marketing, it will drain you, not unless you have a huge budget for marketing alone.

This leads us to the second method, which is to search for low target keywords. By doing low target keywords, this will ensure that somewhat fewer have a placement on the search results for that certain keyword. So, say, your book is about depression. When you searched for the keyword "depression", you saw that the competitors were about 100,000. That's not a low target keyword, that's a high target one. But when you scrolled down for a bit, you saw that the word "dejection" only has about 14 competitors, and the searches per month for this keyword is about 300. That is a good example of a low target keyword. If you use "dejection" on your title or your book description, your book will appear in 300 searches and you only have to fight 14 other books that have the same keyword as you. That's better, compared to fighting 5,000 competitors.

The key here is to choose keywords that have less competition so that you can rank better. This is what most small and medium businesses do, as this is the smarter choice when it comes to marketing. If you do not have a humongous budget for your marketing, better target low traffic keywords as they will ensure that you have a spot on the search results. It doesn't matter if the monthly searches are just 300 for that particular keyword. This simply means that your site will be seen by 300 people every month, so that's 3,600 people every year without you doing anything at all. All you did was put this particular keyword on your title or your book description. Now, imagine if you have 15 low target keywords in your book description. Multiply and add all those, and that's the total possibility of your book showing up on these search results. Amazing, isn't it? That's the power of keywords, and you have it within your reach, so you need to utilize it by all means.

FOREWORD

We have mentioned the foreword, in the previous sections, as one of the parts of the book's front matter, though not all authors prefer to have one. It's a preference, really. Most readers usually skip this part and just proceed with the book's content, however, having one is a boost to your book's marketability and credibility.

When searching for a foreword writer, you cannot just ask your neighbor Joe to write one for you. Sure, you can ask anyone rather than yourself to write one for you, but usually, the people who are asked to write a foreword are known people, and those in the same field or niche as the book itself. Having a celebrity or a known person will help you with your book's endorsement as well.

So how do you find the perfect person for your book's foreword? I will be honest with you here. The searching is simple, but getting a "yes" is hard. As mentioned, you need to find celebrities in your niche to write the foreword. If you have a celebrity friend within your niche, then problem solved! There is no need to look further. You can ask them to write it for you. However, if you don't, you just need to search for the "top 10 known people in X", where X is your niche or field. So, say, your book is about starting a company from the ground. Search for people who are known to guide startup companies.

Now that you have your first 10 people, visit their websites and click on their contact form. It would be awesome to find really big people such as Tony Robbins (for business-related books), but you know that the chances of you getting a "yes" from him are slim to none. So, try to stay away from super-big people. There is no harm in trying though, and you have nothing to lose. Send them an email through their company's contact form, or if they have their email addresses on their websites, then go ahead and send them a personal one. Introduce yourself and your book and ask them if they can write a foreword for you. Don't forget to attach a copy of your book as well. Remember, they are writing a foreword for you, and their forewords are sort of endorsements for your book. They need to know what they are endorsing and these people are not willing to put their names on the line for something that they don't agree with or support.

In your email, also mention good things about them and what you liked about their work. Praise them, but don't overdo it, as that is obsequious. They don't like cringeworthy fanatics, as they have had enough of those from some of their fans.

Now, you know how important time is for these people. Since they are celebrities in their own respective fields, when you visit their website, you will see various upcoming events these people are invited to. Some of them even have daily events, all over the nation, and so, they will view your request as an added nuisance and inconvenience to their schedule. This is expected, and this is also the reason why most of them say no. There is a workaround for this, don't worry. What you can do to save them some time in writing a foreword, is to draft up to three forewords for them, and attach it in your email along with your request message. Most of these celebrity people must have workers underneath them who write their forewords for them, as they get tons of requests from authors like you, but it would be beneficial for them if you have three forewords ready, as this will save them a lot of time. Tell them that they can tweak it however they want to, and as much as they want to. Mention that what you sent them were just drafts to make their lives easier.

Sending them three drafts will not result in a definite "yes". Again, it will depend on the person, and if they want to be a part of your book. If you get a rejection from any of the celebrity people you contacted, don't feel bad. Instead, send them a thank you note back, and move on to the next person. Just keep searching, and use different keywords in your celebrity search. Every time you use a different keyword, different results pop up and all these people are worth contacting. You will never know who in your list would say yes. Remember, all you need is one "yes" from them. You don't need ten or five. Just one. Once you get a yes, then you just opened the doors to greater book endorsements with the celebrity name on your book cover.

The good thing about this is you can put this celebrity's name in your Amazon book page as one of the contributors. They will have the tag "(Foreword)" after their name, and if the celebrity person is also a writer, whenever people search for their name on Amazon and check their published works, your book will also be there on their page. This is free marketing for you!

BOOKSTORES

Apart from having your book on Amazon, it would also be equally great to have your book in some local bookstores. Some readers still prefer the aroma of newly-published books, and generally prefer browsing through hardcovers and paperbacks on shelves, rather than clicking their way through pages of search results. The nostalgia it creates, and the excitement one gets upon seeing hundreds of books on the shelf are still favorable to some old-school bibliophiles. They love it if they have to go through a few aisles of books, and not leave the place until they find that one book they need for their collection.

Having your book in several bookstores alone will probably not make you a bestseller, however, it will definitely add to the tally of sales for your book. It is also a great feeling to see your book being displayed on bookstore cases, not to mention the fact that your reach will widen to communities who have never heard of you before.

Reaching out to other bookstores is easy. You have a hometown, I suppose? You probably are living in an area now far from where you grew up. What you can do is go back to your hometown and introduce yourself to the bookstore owner. The great thing about local bookstores is there no red tape. You can reach the owner of the bookstore right away, and sometimes they are even the ones operating the cash boxes of their businesses. Tell them that you grew up in the area, but have transferred to another state. Talk to them and tell them your story. Be personable to them.

Mention that you recently wrote a book and have published it on Amazon, but would love to have them sell a copy to the readers in the area. Contact bookstores within a 50-mile radius and do the same for all. It's going to be a tedious task, but worth it, knowing that these local bookstores will soon carry your book. Depending on how you approach them, they may or may not agree to feature your book in their bookstore, however, 99% of the time, they would actually say yes. There is no overhead cost for them as they don't need to pre-purchase your book. All they need is a few inches of space on their shelves. These bookstore owners love to support local authors, and if they live in a tight-knit community, the owners oftentimes recommend books to their customers. Who knows? The next recommendation that they might do is your book! Give it a couple of weeks and it will spread like wildfire.

On the other hand, if you don't like small-time bookstores, not that you have anything against them, and wanted bigger bookstore chains such as Barnes & Noble, there is also a way to do it. You can go through the normal process of going through their website, downloading the necessary forms, and submitting your application via email and snail mail.

However, there is an even easier way to do it. All you need to do is contact Authors Unite and they will get your book distributed through Barnes & Noble and all other major retailers for a fee. They have helped over 250 people with their book launches, including known authors such as Christopher Kai and Jolie Dawn. Authors Unite can orchestrate this for you, and you don't even need to submit any forms, or mail anything. They have a "done-for-you" service and will get the job done.

EMAIL LIST

They say the money is in the email list. Even though there are other marketing routes one can take for your book, such as Facebook ads, AMS ads, Google Adwords, nothing beats the power of an email marketing list. Simply put, an email list is a compilation of emails that businesses have gathered throughout time, whether it be from their previous customers, or people who are just interested in their content, products, or services that they are offering. Businesses usually send out an email marketing blast to this list, which is similar to a newsletter, normally composed of new offerings or announcements made by the company (or individual).

Email lists are important to any business because generally speaking, email blasts have a higher click through rate (CTR) compared to paid ads. Why? The reason is simple. These people have either purchased from you in the past or have voluntarily signed up for your newsletter so that they can get announcements from you whenever you send out a blast.

So, how do you start creating a list of your own? You have to start with your website. Imagine your website as a piece of land that you are allowed to design and tinker with. We will discuss in the next section the important parts of an effective website, but before you jump to that, you have to scatter your call to action (CTA) all over your page. Here are a few examples of how you can do it:

- CTA buttons on every landing page, or every section if you have a one-page website
- Pop-ups or slide-ins with images, asking them to subscribe
- Pop-up surveys

At this point, once you have created your CTA buttons and sections, you can use social media to disseminate the information. You can tell them that you have an email newsletter and you can describe what the subscribers will get from your newsletter. You cannot send them spam emails as that is against most of the email platforms' privacy and terms. They are very strict about this and if people keep on reporting you as spam, your account in the email platform of your choosing will be suspended. This also prevents people from purchasing email lists from third party vendors. This is a sad reality and many people do this, but this won't do any good for your account. You may have added 10,000 people on your email list from the list that you have purchased from somewhere, but once these people report you as spam, your account will be closed, not to mention that the list is probably not targeted to your niche, so you won't receive sales from it at all.

The only legit way to get an email list is to build it from scratch by doing the things that we have indicated in this section. With this method, you can ensure that the people who sign up for your email list are genuinely interested in your content.

AUTHOR WEBSITE

We have now reached the author website part, and in this section, you will learn why creating one is equally important as your Amazon book page.

If the Amazon book page is your book's homepage, the author's website is going to be your homepage. Upon reaching your Amazon book page, potential readers will read through your book description and author bio, and since you can only do more or less 200 words for the bio, this is not enough space for people to get to know you better. The website offers a solution to that. With your own website, you can put additional information about you, events that you are going to, speaking invites, links to blogs and your social media account—basically, anything that will make your potential readers know more about you.

Remember, people trust those to whom they can relate more, so if your book is about depression, creating a website that acts as a panacea to what people are looking for will definitely boost your book's legitimacy, and your credibility as an author. Some author websites I have seen in the past have About Me sections that tell a story about their childhood and what, in their childhood, led them to writing a book about their topic. These are relatable stories and people like that.

Now, whether you want to create a one-page or multi-page website is up to you. It really depends on your preference. Multi-pages are more for those who prefer to have the traditional-looking websites, but others actually like one-paged sites because nothing beats simplicity. The more you make people think, the more they veer away from you, and since it's a website, they can just click back on their browser buttons, and you can kiss your potential followers and readers goodbye.

A good website has a clear message. If you want to tell your visitors that you are an experienced yogi (if, say, your book is about meditation), then illustrate that message clearly right away. You can put a picture or a video on your site's hero background of you doing some yoga poses and meditation, as this will show the visitors visually what you actually specialize in. One look and they know that you are a yogi, based on the photos and videos that you have on your site's main background.

Another thing that actually helps is a one-line message on top of your background. This should be a clear and firm message that tells who you are as a person and what you do. This message should be easy to understand since visitors can simply close that tab to your website and forget about you, without even knowing who you are first. This part is as crucial as your book description as this can also make or break your website. People who find your one-line confusing will leave your site right away.

Next, you need to have a couple of testimonials in there from your previous customers or clients. As we have mentioned several times in the past, people love social proof. If you have a lot of testimonials on your site, this can help gain the trust of your visitors, especially if the testimonials are from known people. You have probably seen websites of known people in the past, but even though they are already known in their respective fields, they still put testimonials on their sites, either from other known people or their past clients. This is how important social proof is. It doesn't matter if you are already known in your field, you need a few ones on your site, no matter what.

If, say, you are a speaker on the side, include the logos of institutions that you gave talks to in the past. This is a great way to further boost your social proof. You might have seen sites that display logos of Inc., Entrepreneur, ABC, CNN, Fox and all other prominent institutions in media. If gave a talk in a university in the past, go ahead and add that. If you were invited to become a part of a panel of some company, then add that as well. The more you add on your site, the better. However, if you were invited to 20 or more institutions, for the love of God, do not add everything in there as it will take the entire page, and it will just look like you are gloating. People will get turned off if you get too crass about it.

Also, if you have photos taken with famous people, then you can put them on your site as well. Avoid political people unless your book is political, or if your field is about politics, then do so. However, this might turn off other people if your book is not about politics at all. As much as possible, stay away from sensitive topics such as politics, religion, race, and sexuality. Try to focus on your ; for example, if you are a yoga instructor, post pictures of you and another famous person who does yoga. Or if you are a business person, post pictures of you and another leader in the business world.

Apart from posting logos of institutions that invited you to speak in the past, also include logos of media outlets that have featured you or your story. We have mentioned a few paragraphs before this that some people do this. They put logos of Inc., Entrepreneur, CNN, etc., and they plaster maybe four or five of these on their site. If you do the same, this will make you more trustworthy and people will be more engaged with what you are offering.

Lastly, if you have other published works, you can include that on your site. This is important as this will introduce more people to your other works. If you have written other books, you can market that here and visitors will see all of your work just by visiting your website. This is a creative and subtle way of marketing to your visitors. Just from one book, they visited your author's bio, checked out your website, and knew more about you in just a span of 20 minutes. This is the amazing power of linking on the internet. If you have everything stringed, you will get more visits and people will know more about you in a few clicks or so.

You can also do a little Search Engine Optimization (SEO) on your site so that you can get more organic searches for your site. If you have the budget, hire a copywriter, whether it's a company or an individual, it doesn't matter, as long as it's a professional and one who has done sales pages in the past in the same niche as you. This way, you can ensure that you have written good ranking words on your site, and that whenever people search for some terms on the search engine, your site will pop up on the search results.

NEXT STEPS

Crush your competitors with amazing reviews and keyword research.

- Go to becomingabestseller.com and either create a free account or log in to your existing Path to Publish
- Gather more reviews for your book through:
  - Inner network
  - Signing up on book review sites and picking a package
  - Contacting Goodreads reviews and joining groups
- Purchase Publisher Rocket and research on keywords. Aim to rank high on keywords with less competition.
- Find celebrities in your field/niche and contact them.
  - Draft up to three forewords and send to them
- Reach out to your local bookstores and give them copies
- Start gathering an email list by asking your site visitors for their email addresses
- Create a stunning author website so people will get to know more about you
- Reach out to us if you need more help with any of the steps above by sending an email to coaching@becomingabestseller.com

NOTES

FUNNELS: GUIDING THEM THROUGH THE PROCESS

B y now, you have created a stunning website! Congratulations! However, your job here is not yet done. What good does a stunning website do, if you cannot track what people are doing on your site? You might have a good-looking site, but people leave the moment they get to a certain page. Think of your visitors as kids who are just starting first grade. You have to hold their hand throughout the entire process. Funnels, by definition, is the mapping out of a customer's journey throughout your site. It makes sense, as your site is new to their eyes and they don't know how to navigate through it yet.

Funnels are depicted as an inverted triangle because the entire process includes weeding out those who are not really interested. A total of 20 people could visit your site, but in the end, only two purchase from you.

As the visitors pass from one stage to another, you have to offer them a deeper commitment to whatever it is you're offering, and ultimately, your purchase goal. There are four basic stages for funnels. Some funnels are more complex than others, and that's ok too, but these four are staple in every funnel:

- Understanding
- Interest
- Commitment
- Action

UNDERSTANDING

This stage is all about letting the people know about your product or service. This is where you introduce them to what it is you are offering. In your case, it would be the topic of your book. Say, your topic is marriage counseling. You have to make them aware of this problem and remind them that they need to solve it, and that you have possible ways on how to deal with it.

Remember, this is the first time that visitors see your site, so you have to target their pain right away. Let them know that you are aware of this problem, and can solve the problem for them.

INTEREST

At this stage, the visitor is already actively searching for solutions to their problem. They have acknowledged the problem at this point, and you have to apply pleasure to their pain. This means that you need to show them that you have the solution to their problem and say it in a very clear manner. Any kind of confusion will steer them away and they will exit your website without batting an eyelash. Remember, they have just entered your "space" and they don't know who you are. They have no idea what you can do, and if you are who you say you are. So make the pleasure part fast and clear.

COMMITMENT

At this stage, visitors are now more interested in what you are offering. They are now in your third funnel and are very much committed to what you are offering. This is that they are thinking whether they would fully commit to you or not. They are making the decision of whether they are going to take advantage of your pleasure or solution, or not. They are paying more attention to what you are offering, and this is the time that you have lay out all the packages and options that you have so that the visitor can make the final purchase.

ACTION

This is the final stage and this is where the visitor becomes a full-pledged customer. The customer has purchased a package from you, and has finalized the deal with you. They have made their decision to put their full trust in you by buying your product or service.

In all of your funnels, make sure that you integrate your Facebook ad pixel to it. This code is unique to your ads and what it does is, it collects data that will eventually help you with tracking your conversions from your active ads. You can even use this to remarket to those who have taken action on your site in the past, but want to up-sell them to something else. Apart from this, you can also use the data you have collected to create better Facebook ads if your ads are not doing well.

BESTSELLER LIST

To be included in any bestseller list is a privilege that not all authors enjoy in their lifetime. Some authors that I know have published three to five books already, but have never reached bestselling status in any of them.

Trying to achieve the bestselling status for your book is tricky at best. Though there are a lot of bestselling lists out there, only about three are being regarded as the Holy Grail in the publishing world: New York Times, Wall Street Journal, and USA Today. Why do I say tricky? It's because each bestselling list has their own requirements for them to even consider your book as a bestseller. A good example of this is this one author who has sold over 500,000 copies of her book, but has not been included in the New York Times Bestselling List even if she did better than 99% of her competitors. This is because her book was not published by a big New York publishing house, so NY Times never even considered her book to be a contender for the spot.

So it is important that when you try to achieve bestselling status, you know the requirements for each list. Sales are important, but sometimes not enough for you to be included in their list.

However, it does make sense for all authors to dream about becoming a bestselling one. It is a necessary evil for some, since it helps them boost their status in the publishing industry, as well as their credibility for their readers. Try picking up a book from your local bookstore that has a "#1 bestselling author" sprawled on the book cover. Aren't you more intrigued with this book than the rest?

Despite the tedious work that authors have to go through, and the things they have to consider to become a bestseller, some authors still strive to be a part of the list.

Becoming a part of the list is a status symbol. If your book has been a part of the bestselling list, then you can republish a revised version of your book cover and include in bold letters, "#1 bestselling author". This will boost your status as an author, and will make your book stand out from the rest of the bunch on the shelf. Also, if you have other careers such as career coach or motivational speaker, having a bestselling book will add to your credibility, and will probably get you more speaking engagements and clients in the future.

TWO REQUIREMENTS OF BECOMING A BESTSELLER

Even though each bestseller list has different requirements, there are two universal principles that apply to them all: 1) How fast you sell your book at a given time, and 2) reporting.

HOW FAST YOU SELL

To be honest, the amount of books that you sell is not enough to put you in the bestseller list. You may sell 10,000 copies in a year, but this is not enough to be a part of any bestselling list. It's pretty impressive though, but just not enough. However, if you sell 10,000 copies in a week, then you may have a chance to hit a lot of bestselling lists out there.

This is the key when it comes to becoming a bestseller. It's not just about the amount of sales, really, but the amount of sales in a given time. The timeframe depends on the bestseller list, but the faster you sell more books in a short amount of time, the better it is.

Selling 10,000 copies a year is hard enough to do, and selling 10,000 copies a week is even more difficult, this is why achieving that bestselling status is ridiculously hard.

To achieve this feat, some authors create a following first before they release their book, and then at the time of the launch, they release their books to their followers, who have probably already waited for weeks to get a copy of it. If they have 1,000 followers, then this would mean 1,000 downloads on the first two to three days from the date of release, which is astonishing!

This is also the reason why having a fixed release date for your book, and concentrating your marketing around that date, is crucial. You can spend the bulk of your marketing budget on your book launch, and market it to different media, from social media to local ads.

REPORTING OF SALES IS IMPORTANT

There is no such thing as a real bestseller list. What do I mean by that? It means that there is no overall bestseller list since all these bestselling lists have different criteria in terms of what books will make the cut for bestseller per week.

For example, the Amazon bestseller list only counts books that have sold the most at a given time through their website. The New York Times bestseller list only counts books that have been sold the most in both physical and a few online stores.

So, if you want to reach bestselling status for a particular list, then make sure that you know how they calculate what is a bestseller, as not all lists have the same criteria. Once you know what list to target, then make sure that you focus on that list alone.

KNOW THE RULES OF EACH BESTSELLER LIST

I can't reiterate enough that you need to know all the criteria of the list that you are targeting. Some bestseller lists only consider books from certain categories, and if your book is not classified under that category, even though you sell 1,000,000 copies in an hour, you still won't be considered a bestseller. So to make is easier for you, we have compiled here a list of the biggest bestseller lists in the publishing world. We have also included the guidelines for each list, so that you can prepare better.

NEW YORK TIMES BESTSELLER LIST

This is the top bestseller list of all lists—the Holy Grail of all bestseller lists. It is a privilege to be a part of this, and only a few authors have graced this list. Some of them such as Stephen King, JK Rowling, and the like, have been an NY Times bestseller numerous times already, so if you become a part of this list, you can consider yourself part of the top tier authors out there.

According to NY Times, they calculate the bestsellers from Monday of the previous week, to Monday of the current week. On their website, it reads[31]:

"Rankings reflect sales reported by vendors offering a wide range of general interest titles. The sales venues for print books include independent book retailers; national, regional and local chains; online and multimedia entertainment retailers; super-markets, university, gift and discount department stores; and newsstands. E-book rankings reflect sales from leading online vendors of e-books in a variety of popular e-reader formats.

E-book sales are presently included for all adult categories (fiction, non-fiction and advice) except for graphic novels, and all children's categories with the exception of picture books. Titles are included regardless of whether they are published in both print and electronic formats or just one format. E-books available exclusively from a single vendor will be tracked at a future date."

To explain this further, NY Times is actually a survey list, and they do not really rely on the total number of sales in total. They already have a selected few booksellers, who they monitor every week, and that is how they tabulate the results. Independent bookstores do weigh more for them, since they think indie bookstore buyers are the more serious buyers than the rest.

They also take into consideration the amount of books one person buys, and they don't count those who buy books in bulk. This prevents authors from buying in bulk just to hit the list, so if you're thinking of purchasing 1,000 copies of your book just to spike the numbers, then you're wrong. NY Times doesn't count book sales this way. If you are a speaker and are planning to give away your book, but purchase it from the bookstore just to add to the weekly numbers, then you might as well give them free copies instead because this is still considered bulk buying.

Also, have you noticed that they actually said, "E-books available exclusively from a single vendor will be tracked at a future date." They are pertaining to Amazon when they included this in their guidelines. NY Times, as snobbish as they are, have only recently considered ebook sales in their list. In the past, they didn't even believe that ebooks were "real" books! But now, yes they do count them, but they count them as less.

To be considered as an NY Times bestselling author, you must:

- Not be self-published. Your book should be published by a traditional publishing company, and not all publishing companies are considered, so you have to do your research first before having your book published by your chosen publisher as you might get rid of your chances of becoming an NY Times bestseller because of this.
- Have chosen the correct category for your book, and have a good amount of sales for a given time. NY Times requires their bestsellers to have at least 5,000 book

sales for one week, however, bump it up to 10,000 just to be sure.

- Ask your publisher about the publishing down time to ensure that you have a shot at becoming a bestseller. Publishing companies know the schedule of the down times, so the fewer the books that you compete with, the better it is for you to grab that spot in the bestseller list.

WALL STREET JOURNAL BESTSELLER LIST

This list is not as prestigious as NY Times, however, for business books, this is a great list to target. They are not as snobbish as NY Times in terms of their criteria, but they also have similar impacts in terms of boosting the author's credibility.

According to their website[32]:

"Nielsen BookScan gathers point-of-sale book data from more than 16,000 locations across the U.S., representing about 85% of the nation's book sales. Print-book data providers include all major booksellers (now inclusive of Wal-Mart) and Web retailers, and food stores. E-book data providers include all major e-book retailers (Apple excepted). Free e-books and those sold for less than 99 cents are excluded. The fiction and nonfiction lists in all formats include both adult and juvenile titles; the business list includes only adult titles. The combined lists track sales by title across all print and e-book formats; audio books are excluded."

As you can see, the WSJ bestseller list is more reasonable and fair than NY Times. They get their data from Nielsen BookScan, which is a data provider for point-of-sale books across 16,000 locations in the US. They have also included Wal-Mart and other web retailers, which is totally the opposite of what NY Times is doing.

To be considered as a Wall Street Journal bestselling author:

- You must sell as many as 3,000 to 5,000 copies.
- If you have opted for a non-traditional publishing company, then you can still be a part of the WSJ bestselling list. They don't discriminate like NY Times.
- Just hit the sales target and remember, just like NY Times, bulk sales are not counted by them, so don't buy your way in to the WSJ list.

USA TODAY BESTSELLER LIST

To be honest, this is not a great list to target alone. It is not as prestigious as NY Times and WSJ, but it is still one of the available bestseller lists out there that authors try to target. Their data used to be pulled solely from Nielsen BookScan, however, they have recently changed that and have started creating a curated list, similar to NY Times. The only difference is, both NY Times and WSJ rank the books per category, however USA Today puts all books into one category and ranks them from there.

On their website, they have described their methodology as[33]:

"Each week, USA TODAY collects sales data from booksellers representing a variety of outlets: bookstore chains, independent bookstores, mass merchandisers, and online retailers. Using that data, we determine the week's 150 top-selling titles. The first 50 are published in the print version of USA TODAY each Thursday. The top 150 are published online. The rankings reflect sales from the previous Monday through Sunday.

USA TODAY's Best-Selling Books list is a ranking of titles selling well each week at a broad range of retail outlets. It reflects combined sales of titles in print and electronic format, if available. For example, if Jane Austen's Pride and Prejudice sells copies in hardcover, paperback and e-book during a particular week, sales from each format are combined to determine its rank. The description of a title and the publisher name refers to the version selling the most copies in a particular week— hardcover (H), paperback (P) and e-book (E)."

To be considered as a USA Today bestselling author:

- There is no number of sales really, as they only rank the top 50 (or 150 for the online version) from book sales. This means that the more you sell, the better it is.
- Before, USA Today included things like cookbooks and maps in their bestseller list, though as of the current time, they have pulled them off, so that they could focus more on "real" books like novels, etc.

AMAZON BESTSELLER LIST

The Amazon bestseller list is by far the easiest list to get on to. Amazon computes for the top 100 sellers of books on their site. They update the list hourly, and the list is basically a popularity contest—which books sell the most every hour.

Their methodology is simple. They compute for pure sales on their platform, and based on their algorithm, they rank you based on your trailing sales. If you sell 20 books in an hour, and no sales come in after that, you won't fall off the list just like that. You will go down the rankings and keep falling, until you start selling more of your book.

To be considered as a USA Today bestselling author:

- You have to concentrate all your marketing efforts on the launch date.
- You should have more or less 500 sales on your launch date to make it to the top 100 list.
- If you want to hit top 10, you have to make about 2,000 sales.
- If you want to hit #1 in one subcategory, it's different than overall top 100 or 10. You just need a few sales.
- Don't purchase 1,000 of your book to be included in the system. In short, don't game the system. Amazon is a huge company and they know better. They track IP addresses and credit card purchases, and they will punish you if they catch you cheating.

COMPANIES THAT HELP YOU GET TO THE LIST

Not unless you have a huge budget (and I cannot stress this enough), you can opt for companies that offer ways in to the bestseller list. The fees included are just ridiculously hefty, and we're talking about something like $200,000 just for New York Times alone (that is the minimum!). But I can assure you that there are some books in the bestseller lists now that have bought their way in by hiring these big companies to help them get that top spot. If you have the budget, then go for it!

NEXT STEPS

Make use of funnels to understand your customers more.

- Go to becomingabestseller.com and either create a free account or log in to your existing Path to Publish
- Start with a simple funnel that consists of four steps. You can expand on it later on:
  - Understanding _____

    _____
  - Interest _____

    _____
  - Commitment _____

    _____
  - Action _____

    _____

- Target a bestseller list based on your budget. Read their requirements to ensure that you qualify for the list before you start with it.
- If you want a proven funnel that works for any kind of genre, talk to us by sending us an email at coaching@becomingabestseller.com and we will help you create an effective funnel.

NOTES

PURE PROFIT: TAKING IT TO THE NEXT LEVEL

We are finally at the last part of our book and this is perhaps the part that will make you different from all the other bestsellers out there. Yes, you have achieved the bestseller status, but so did other people. How you use this bestseller status to your advantage will make the difference. Some people stop after becoming a bestseller, and this is the sad part because they have so much potential and their bestseller status could have led to something bigger, but they decided to stop at that. Again, it depends on your goal. If your book was just a passion project, then all the other things don't matter, but if your goal is for branding purposes, then becoming a bestseller is just the beginning of your journey.

DONE-FOR-YOU SERVICE

There are a few things that you can do after becoming a bestseller. First, you can do a "done-for-you" service. This type of service is very common for service-oriented companies or individuals, as they offer shortcuts to success. They are well-sought-out by those who are not so technical, and those who don't have the time to do the nitty-gritty things that we have just discussed in the previous sections. You'd be shocked at how well these done-for-you services are selling.

The selling point of this kind of service is the idea that those who purchase your package will have the same exact template that worked for you in the past. Who can let go of that opportunity? If people see that it worked for you, then there is a huge chance that it will work for them. It's the same template, after all. It's like their hand is being held the entire time during this process, and they love it. The fact is that they know that your system is proven to succeed, and a lot of research hours have been put into it, so copying your system will result in nothing but success.

CONSULTING

Another option is to start a consulting business for your book topic. I have seen quite a few authors take this path, to be honest. They publish a book, make it a bestseller, and then offer services related to their book topic. On their sales pages, you would see that they are using this bestselling book as leverage for people to trust them more. They mention on their site that they have a bestselling book, and this seems to boost their credibility because not everyone knows how to become a bestseller! This is such a huge deal for them. The same goes for you. If you have a book on helping women fight patriarchy, then you can offer a service that empowers women. You can include different packages on your website, and offer programs with different value amounts. You can even include a "supreme" package, wherein they can opt for a one or two-hour consultation with you. This format is what we call a high-ticket service, which normally costs a minimum of $2,000. Now imagine getting 100, or even 50 bookings for this package! That's a guaranteed $100,000 in your bank account! An ordinary person would need to work more than 365 days to earn this money, but with your consulting business in place, you would only need a few months to get this amount.

ONLINE COURSE AND
MEMBERSHIP SITE

The next option is to offer an online course on your site. Have you seen sites that offer modules wherein people can sign up for the course, and after being given access to it, they can take the course at their own pace? That is exactly what we're talking about. If you think these kinds of courses don't sell, you're wrong. They do, especially if the course is something that the people want. Udemy is a known platform that offers a multitude of courses. They have been doing this for a decade, and the number of their students is growing. It is because they target adults who don't have time to go to a traditional class, and learn all the things they want to learn. An accountant can learn how to code Python on Udemy for as low as $200, and this accountant doesn't even need to register at a university, or even take entrance exams just to learn how to code Python. It's an amazing platform and people love it.

The principle is the same with Udemy, but the only difference is that you will not be selling your course for $10, $50, or $200. You will price your course between $300 and $1999, and this is what we call low-ticket service. The great news about this is you won't have to deal with consultation calls, unlike the high-ticket service that we mentioned earlier, as everything is pretty much recorded. We are in the 21st century, and what good are the technological advances that we have right now if we are not going to use them to make money, right? All your content, tips, tricks, materials will be delivered either through video or digital download. You can definitely include phone calls if you want to, as a personal touch, but there is no need to do that. Most people only do phone calls as a way of re-targeting people. If you are up-selling your viewers to another package, and you have a list of those who purchased the membership course, but did not push through with your high-ticket offering, then you can call them to find out what happened along the way. This is the beauty of online courses. Once you have created your course, you're done! You don't need to do anything else, really, content-wise.

On the other hand, a membership site is when you have people sign up on your site, charge them a monthly fee and continuously deliver amazing content every week, month or whatever your promised timeline is. If, say, you have a podcast site or a blog about your book topic, and you create content on a regular basis, or interview special people every month or so, then a membership site is the more appropriate for you. Though it is true that membership sites take less effort to start than online courses, it actually takes a lot more effort to sustain them over time. This is because membership sites usually deliver content gradually, compared to online courses' "one-time, big time" mantra of dumping all the information into one course. Because of this, since you will be producing less content for membership sites, it's much less effort, but you have to keep your content interesting so that people will continue to pay the monthly fee that you charge them. They have to feel that you are giving them value based on the content you're releasing.

WHICH IS THE RIGHT FORMAT FOR YOU?

Both are great, in terms of gathering new leads and getting your name out there, however, you really have to consider time and effort if you are confused which format to adopt. Below are the differences in tabular form, so it's easier for you to know the differences:

Online Course	Membership Site
If you want to dump all your content into one space, and don't want to generate content on a regular basis, then go for an online course.	If you want to gradually build an audience by publishing content on a regular basis, then go for a membership site.
If you want to sell your content in one package, like an all-in-one product, then go for an online course.	If you want to grow your revenue over time, then go for a membership site.

SPEAKING

Lastly, if you are into branding and are accepting speaking engagements, your book is your calling card. Once people see on your site that you are a bestseller, they will reach out more to you, and will ask you to talk more about your field or your book topic. This is an amazing opportunity for you to get your name out there. Put on your site that you are accepting speaking invites about your topic, and because of your bestselling book, people will then view you as an expert. You can create speeches based on your book, and you can start reaching out to conference coordinators by telling them who you are, and as an added touch, you can even include a free copy of your book so that they, too, can enjoy the masterpiece that you have created.

Take your profit to the next level.

- Go to becomingabestseller.com and either create a free account or log in to your existing Path to Publish
- Think what format/platform works for you:
    - Done-for-You Services
    - Consulting Business
    - Online course or Membership site
    - Speaking
- Start creating your content based on the platform that you chose.
- Shoot videos if you are going to webinars, and make sure that the video quality is good.
- Remember to be organized when gathering content.
- If you want us to assist you in taking your business to the next level, send us an email at coaching@becomingabestseller.com and we will be more than happy to do it with you.

SOURCES

1. Rodela, J. (n.d.). Boost Online Sales with Product Reviews. Retrieved from https://www.business.com/articles/77-percent-of-people-read-online-reviews-before-buying-are-they-finding-you/

2. Pierson, G. (2010, June 21). The Power of Social Proof. Retrieved from https://www.searchenginejournal.com/the-power-of-social proof/21896/

3. Simon, S. (2010, October 18). The Secret to Turning Consumers Green. Retrieved from http://online.wsj.com/article/SB10001424052748704575304575296243891721972.html

4. Wikipedia. (2019, April 16). The Seven Basic Plots. Retrieved from https://en.wikipedia.org/wiki/The_Seven_Basic_Plots

5. Flood, A. (2015, April 20). Median earnings of professional authors fall below the minimum wage. Retrieved from https://www.theguardian.com/books/2015/apr/20/earnings-authors-below-minimum-wage

6. A quote by Will Smith. (n.d.). Retrieved from https://www.goodreads.com/quotes/830842-fear-is-not-real-the-only-place-that-fear-can

7. Wikipedia. (2019, May 05). Fear. Retrieved from https://en.wikipedia.org/wiki/Fear

8. Les Brown "Ghosts" Speech. (2016, May 29). Retrieved from https://motivationalwisdomblog.wordpress.com/2016/05/29/les-brown-ghosts-speech/

9. A quote by George R.R. Martin. (n.d.). Retrieved from https://www.goodreads.com/quotes/749309-i-think-there-are-two-types-of-writers-the-architects

10. A quote by George R.R. Martin. (n.d.). Retrieved from https://www.goodreads.com/quotes/749309-i-think-there-are-two-types-of-writers-the-architects

11. CNN. (n.d.). Mandela in his own words. Retrieved from http://edition.cnn.com/2008/WORLD/africa/06/24/mandela.quotes/

12. Howes, L. (2012, July 19). 20 Lessons from Walt Disney on Entrepreneurship, Innovation and Chasing Your Dreams. Retrieved from https://www.forbes.com/sites/lewishowes/2012/07/17/20-business-quotes-and-lessons-from-walt-disney/#3a1d3f7a4ba9

13. SUBRAMANIAN, G. (2019, May 07). What is BATNA? How to Find Your Best Alternative to a Negotiated Agreement. Retrieved from https://www.pon.harvard.edu/daily/batna/translate-your-batna-to-the-current-deal/

14. Corissajoy. (2016, June 29). Zone of Possible Agreement (ZOPA). Retrieved from https://www.beyondintractability.org/essay/zopa

15. Clifford, C. (2018, June 11). Ex-FBI hostage negotiator: This is what you can expect from President Trump and Kim Jong Un summit. Retrieved from https://cnbc.com/2018/06/11/ex-fbi-hostage-negotiator-chris-voss-on-donald-trump-kim-jong-un.html

16. Charzuk, M. (n.d.). Video Lessons & Resources. Retrieved from https://www.acx.com/help/recording/202008280

17. Charzuk, M. (n.d.). Video Lessons & Resources. Retrieved from https://www.acx.com/help/mastering/202008300

18. Malbon, A. (2018, October 10). Kylie Jenner has decided to get lip fillers again after having them removed. Retrieved from https://www.cosmopolitan.com/uk/beauty-hair/a23698519/kylie-jenner-lip-fillers-again-after-removed/

19. Blank, A. (2010, July 22). Teen barters phone for a Porsche convertible. Retrieved from http://edition.cnn.com/2010/LIVING/07/22/teen.barter.cell.porsche/index.html

20. Walsh, J. (n.d.). The 4-Hour Workweek by Tim Ferriss. Retrieved from https://www.joshwalsh.com/library/the-4-hour-workweek

21. Billingsley, D. (n.d.). Vivid Vision: A Remarkable Tool For Aligning Your Business Around a Shared Vision of the. Retrieved from https://darylbillingsley.com/books/vivid-vision-a-remarkable-tool-for-aligning-your-business-around-a-shared-vision-of-the/

22. Tan, B. (n.d.). Retrieved from https://experal.com/marketplace/the-hard-thing-about-hard-things-building-a-business-when-there-are-no-easy-answers-1544058533090

23. Penguin Random House Canada. (n.d.). Coercion by Douglas Rushkoff. Retrieved from https://www.penguinrandomhouse.ca/books/348346/coercion-by-douglas-rushkoff/9781573228299

24. Penguin Random House. (n.d.). Timothy Ferriss | Penguin Random House. Retrieved from https://www.penguinrandomhouse.com/authors/75629/timothy-ferriss

25. WILD MOUNTAIN MEMOIR. (2012, November 27). Keynote: Cheryl Strayed. Retrieved from https://wildmountainmemoir.wordpress.com/keynote-guest/

26. Leading Expert on Gluten Intolerance & Allergies — Dr. Perlmutter. (n.d.). Retrieved from https://www.drperlmutter.com/about/

27. FaithGateway. (n.d.). Dr. Ben Carson, Author at FaithGateway. Retrieved from https://www.faithgateway.com/author/ben-carson/

28. Christianbook.com, LLC. (n.d.). Heaven Is for Real: A Little Boy's Astounding Story of His Trip to Heaven and Back, Deluxe Edition. Retrieved from https://www.christianbook.com/heaven-little-astounding-story-deluxe-edition/todd-burpo/9780849948367/pd/948367#CBD-PD-Description

29. Dogberry Pages. (n.d.). The Big Short by Michael Lewis. Retrieved from http://books.dogberrypatch.com/book-info/big-short-michael-lewis/

30. Powhatan County, VA. (n.d.). Retrieved from http://www.powhatanva.gov/1548/Books-More

31. Johnson City Public Library. (n.d.). Readers Resources. Retrieved from https://www.jcpl.org/adultreaders-resources/

32. Wall Street Journal. (2016, November 04). Best-Selling Books Week Ended Oct. 30. Retrieved from https://www.wsj.com/articles/best-selling-books-week-ended-oct-30-1478278432

33. Usatoday. (2018, October 03). About the Best-Selling Books list. Retrieved from https://www.usatoday.com/story/life/books/2013/06/04/about-usa-todays-best-selling-book-list/2389075/

Made in the USA
Las Vegas, NV
02 October 2024

96219880R00138